Noah Knowles Davis

Elements of inductive Logic

Noah Knowles Davis
Elements of Inductive Logic
ISBN/EAN: 9783743347625

Manufactured in Europe, USA, Canada, Australia, Japa

Cover: Foto ©ninafisch / pixelio.de

Manufactured and distributed by brebook publishing software (www.brebook.com)

Noah Knowles Davis

Elements of Inductive Logic

ELEMENTS

OF

INDUCTIVE LOGIC

BY

NOAH K. DAVIS, Ph.D., LL.D.

PROFESSOR OF MORAL PHILOSOPHY IN THE UNIVERSITY OF VIRGINIA
AND AUTHOR OF "THE THEORY OF THOUGHT"
"ELEMENTS OF DEDUCTIVE LOGIC" ETC.

"Ὅτι *scientiæ fundamentum est,* διότι *fastigium*

NEW YORK
HARPER & BROTHERS PUBLISHERS
1895

Copyright, 1895, by HARPER & BROTHERS.

All rights reserved.

PREFACE

IN preparing the present treatise, I have kept in view the need of collegians and of graduate students in the universities, and endeavored to furnish them with a satisfactory hand-book on Induction. The few pages in popular treatises on Deductive Logic usually allotted to this co-ordinate branch being utterly inadequate and disproportionate, and thereby greatly underrating its extent and importance, should be replaced by a separate treatise comprehending at least the essential elements of Induction, and opening the way for its full investigation and application. In the hope of supplying this want, I offer to students well advanced in the schools the work in hand.

Special students engaged in the pursuit of physical science, who have not enjoyed a full course in Logic, need a compact hand-book on Induction, in order to gain a clearer insight into the principles of the methods they are employing, and thus to avoid a waste of energy, and the discouragement of blunders in the dark. To this class of students, also, and to the general reader who desires a clearer knowledge of his own mental processes and of those of the scientist skilled in the discovery of truth, my work is hopefully addressed.

With these ends in view, I have earnestly tried, first of all, to be true in matter, then clear and distinct in its treatment. Whoever is acquainted with the literature of the subject will recognize my helps, and will, at the same time, accord to me some fair measure of independence. A profusion of illustration has been used, drawn largely from the humbler departments of knowledge, yet in many cases taken from the physical sciences, not for display, but for service, avoiding recondite examples, the purpose being to teach, not physics, but Logic.

The text in the larger type is for the tyro. The many marginal notes, which have been added with much pains, are for the scholarly reader who desires further information. The abundant references to authorities not only indicate my own sources, but will serve to direct those interested to wider fields. As some acquaintance with Deduction is prerequisite to the understanding of Induction, I have ventured to make references to my "Elements of Deductive Logic," the companion of the present work, also a few to "The Theory of Thought," and to my "Elements of Psychology." I ask indulgence for these references, trusting that the bad taste will be neutralized by their helpfulness to those who may have the books at hand.

To Professor Collins Denny, of Vanderbilt University, I am gratefully indebted for encouragement, and for very many valuable suggestions.

NOAH K. DAVIS.

UNIVERSITY OF VIRGINIA.

CONTENTS

I.—DEFINITION

                                                               Page

§ 1. Logic defined and divided 1
§ 2. In both branches a science of forms................. 1
§ 3. Induction distinguished from deduction and defined.. 4
§ 4. Induction synthetic in extension and intension........ 7
§ 5. Analytic judgments distinguished 8
§ 6. Induction a generalization from experience 10
§ 7. Pure truths distinguished from empirical 11
§ 8. Induction a generalization beyond experience 14
§ 9. Summary or closed generalization distinguished...... 15
§ 10. Identification to establish a minor distinguished 16
§ 11. Search after causal relation distinguished 19
§ 12. The definition adequate and real 21

II.—PRINCIPLES

§ 13. Additional principles requisite for induction.......... 22
§ 14. General meaning of cause and condition 22
§ 15. No simple cause or effect. Preventive cause......... 24
§ 16. Theoretic view. Definitions of cause and effect...... 25
§ 17. Recent scientific view of causation.................. 27
§ 18. The principle or axiom of change................... 29
§ 19. The first principle or axiom of uniformity............ 31
§ 20. Plurality of effects, its maxim. Joint effects 33
§ 21. The second principle or axiom of uniformity.......... 35
§ 22. Plurality of causes, its maxim. Resultant motion.... 37
§ 23. Uniformity of nature. The axioms compared........ 39

III.—PROCESS

§ 24. An inductive inference exemplified.................. 41
§ 25. Its conformity to the definition and axioms.......... 41
§ 26. Its immediate character. Formulas................. 43
§ 27. Aristotle's inductive syllogism examined............. 44
§ 28. Hamilton's inductive syllogism criticised............. 46
§ 29. Whately's and Mill's syllogism criticised............. 47
§ 30. General objections to the syllogistic view 48
§ 31. The function and application of forms............... 50
§ 32. Induction immediate. Preparatory process.......... 51

IV.—OBSERVATION

§ 33. Phenomena of coexistence and of succession.......... 54
§ 34. Observation illustrated. Its two modes............. 55
§ 35. Simple observation. Its application................ 57
§ 36. Experimental observation. Its prerogatives.......... 59

V.—ENUMERATION

§ 37. Description. Two kinds of enumeration 62
§ 38. Canon and formula of enumeration of cases.......... 63
§ 39. The justification of this form of induction........... 64
§ 40. Its practical and scientific value 66
§ 41. Analogy distinguished from metaphor, and described.. 67
§ 42. Canon and formula of enumeration of marks......... 69
§ 43. Justification and limitation of analogy. Examples... 71
§ 44. Its practical and scientific value.................... 73

VI.—PROBABILITY

§ 45. Certainty discriminated. Range of probability....... 76
§ 46. Practical importance of probable estimates.......... 78
§ 47. Significance of exceptional cases.................... 80
§ 48. Chance occurrence and concurrence................. 82
§ 49. Calculation of chance. Two special cases........... 84
§ 50. Separation of casual from causal phenomena. Canon. 88
§ 51. The elimination of chance concurrences............. 91
§ 52. The general valuation of probabilities................ 94
§ 53. Their numerical valuation. Statistics 98

VII.—DIFFERENCE

Page
- § 54. Scientific or perfect induction. Canon 102
- § 55. Methods of determining causal relations 103
- § 56. The Method of Difference. Canon and formula 105
- § 57. Examples of the method from simple observation 107
- § 58. Examples from experimental observation. Tests 109
- § 59. Formulas of induction and deduction 111
- § 60. The Method of Residue. Canon and formula 112
- § 61. Examples of discovery by this method 114

VIII.—AGREEMENT

- § 62. The Method of Agreement. Canon and formula 116
- § 63. Examples of the application of this method 118
- § 64. General precautions relative to the methods 120
- § 65. Imperfection of the method of agreement 122
- § 66. Its results only probable. Its scientific value 123
- § 67. The Method of Double Agreement. Canon and formula 125
- § 68. Illustration of its application. Its prerogatives 127
- § 69. A standard example, the research on dew 128

IX.—CONCOMITANCE

- § 70. Method of Concomitant Variations. Canon and formula 130
- § 71. Illustration of its application and insufficiency 132
- § 72. Examples of direct and inverse concomitance 133
- § 73. Measurement of quantity, the mark of advanced science 135
- § 74. The service of this method in developing a science ... 137
- § 75. Three limitations to a mathematical induction 138

X.—DEDUCTION

- § 76. Deductions subsequent to induction. Discovery 141
- § 77. Deductions precedent. Two classes of effects 146
- § 78. The Method of Deduction. Canon and formula 148
- § 79. Three stages in the procedure. Example 151

XI.—HYPOTHESIS

	Page
§ 80. The universal use of supposition or hypothesis	155
§ 81. Supposition involved in all the methods of science	158
§ 82. Formal use of hypothesis in the deductive method	160
§ 83. Definition of scientific hypothesis	162
§ 84. Hypothesis of cause with known law. *Vera causa*	162
§ 85. Hypothesis of law with known cause. Other forms	165
§ 86. Rival hypotheses. *Instantiæ crucis*	168
§ 87. Verification alone not proof. Power of prediction	169
§ 88. Proof of an hypothesis, two steps. Illustrated	171
§ 89. Example of the use of this method by Newton	174

XII.—NATURAL LAW

§ 90. General definition of law	177
§ 91. Formal and material law	178
§ 92. Moral and natural law	179
§ 93. Distribution of natural law	182
§ 94. Empirical laws of coexistence	183
§ 95. Empirical laws of succession	185
§ 96. Rational derivative laws. Examples	187
§ 97. Explanation in its philosophical sense	190
§ 98. Laws of Nature. Examples	193
§ 99. Inductive sciences becoming deductive	197
§ 100. The number of the ultimate Laws of Nature	199
INDEX	201

ELEMENTS OF
INDUCTIVE LOGIC

I.—DEFINITION

§ 1. **Logic is the science of the necessary forms of thought.** This is the definition of pure logic as distinguished from modified and from applied logic, and from what is called material logic. Pure logic, or simply logic, is divided primarily into Deductive Logic and Inductive Logic. The specific difference between these will come to light as we proceed. The latter only is the subject of the present treatise.

§ 2. In undertaking to expound the theory of induction, it is important to state and insist at the outset that the limitation to forms of thought is as proper to this branch of logic as it is to deduction. A number of writers on logic take a contrary view, holding that Deductive Logic is formal, Inductive Logic material; the one having to do subjectively with the laws of thought, the other objectively with the laws of things; the one being the logic of consistency, the other the logic of truth, especially of science; the one being *a priori*, the other *a posteriori* in the sense that it considers the character of individual things or their classes, and thence rises by induction to their laws. These striking antitheses are not justifiable. It is impossible to treat of any matter unless in some form; the laws of thought accord with and lead to the laws of things, as every natural realist maintains; each branch must require self-consistency and be truth-giving, else it is worthless; and the theory of induction, as well as that of deduction, is *a priori*, since it likewise demonstrates its canons, starting from axiomatic principles (§ *4*).[1]

There are other writers on logic who take an extreme view, holding that both Deductive and Inductive Logic are material, that logic in general is an empirical and not a formal science, having to do with things and laws of things rather than with forms and laws of thought.[2]

[1] The reference is to the companion treatise entitled "Elements of Deductive Logic" (Harper & Brothers). See a discussion of the several terms of the definition of Logic in Chapter I. of its Introduction. References to that treatise are in Italics. Figures in Roman type (as, § 25) relate to the present treatise.

[2] Writers adhering to the school of material logicians, if it may be so called, usually claim Mr. J. S. Mill as its founder. Prominent among them is Mr. Venn, notably in his "Empirical Logic." Elsewhere he says: "With what may be called the Material view of Logic, as opposed to the Formal or Conceptualist—with that which regards it as taking cognizance of laws of Things and not of the laws of our own minds in thinking about things—I am in entire accordance."—*Logic*

But logic, throughout both deduction and induction, treats only of form, regardless of matter. To consider the matter of thought in either branch would, as Aristotle says, require omniscience, for sciences are possibly infinite; but the forms of thought being few can be comprised in a single treatise, and being the same for all varieties of matter, they alone need to be studied in their abstract generality in order to discover the necessary processes by which truth is attained (§ 5). This, then, is the sole province of logic: To unfold the formal principles and deduce from them the formal laws by which we think material things and their laws.[1]

of Chance, Preface, p. x. Afterward (ch. x., § 2) he quotes with approbation Mr. Mill's saying that the conceptualist view is "one of the most fatal errors ever introduced into the philosophy of Logic."— Mill, *Logic*, p. 74 (Harper's ed.). For a detailed exposition of Mr. Mill's views, see his "Examination of Hamilton's Philosophy," ch. xx. Mr. Venn, notwithstanding his emphatic endorsement of Mr. Mill, gives us an elaborate work on "Symbolic Logic," which is necessarily and essentially formal throughout; and Mr. Mill in one place very truly says: "The business of Inductive Logic is to provide rules and models (such as the Syllogism and its rules are for ratiocination) to which, if inductive arguments conform, those arguments are conclusive, and not otherwise."—*Logic*, p. 308. Moreover, both Mr. Venn and Mr. Mill in all their logical writings are constantly, and though inconsistently yet happily, occupied with an exposition of the forms of thought, illustrated by material examples. Otherwise, indeed, these writings would not be merely on Logic, but *de omnibus rebus et quibusdam aliis.* The obscurity which seems to cling so strangely and persistently in these latter days to the Aristotelic distinction between the form and the matter of thought, is very remarkable.

[1] As Logic treats of the forms of thought, so Grammar treats of the forms of speech, and Rhetoric of the forms of style. See Hamilton, *Discussions*, article Logic, p. 139 (Harper's ed.).

It should henceforth be clearly and constantly noted that the various technical terms used in treating induction are names of forms, or second intentions. Some of these are : *judgment* and *proposition, genus* and *species, inference, syllogism, phenomenon, circumstance, instance* or *case, cause* and *effect, antecedent* and *consequent, experience, observation, generalization, uniformity, law.* As elsewhere, however, we shall here also freely use material examples and illustrations in first intentions or names of things, that the reader, while never failing to distinguish the form from the matter, may be enabled to grasp more firmly the form by means of concrete matter embodying it (§ *6*).

§ 3. Judgments are primarily of two kinds, intuitions and inferences (§ *77*). Intuitions are self-evident, necessary judgments, and are divided into empirical and pure. In these all knowledge has its beginning; they determine all other judgments. Inferences are enunciations in which from something laid down and admitted, something distinct from what is laid down follows of necessity.[1] To infer,

---

[1] It has been questioned whether this Aristotelic definition of Syllogism, "Analyt. Prior," i., 1, will, as to its last term "of necessity," apply to inductive, as it unquestionably does to deductive, inference. Alexander of Aphrodisias, the Exegete (200 A. D.), in his "Schol. ad Topica," p. 253, intimates that Aristotle included necessary sequence in this definition for the specific purpose of distinguishing deduction by syllogism from induction, a sequence that is not necessary. This view has been generally adopted. But necessity here means only that one cannot grant the premises and deny the conclusion without contra-

then, is to derive a judgment from one or more premised judgments. Inferences also are of two kinds, deductive and inductive.

Deductive inferences are judgments having a generality equal to or less than the premises from which they are derived. We may proceed deductively from *all* to *all*, from *some* to *some*, and from *all* to *some*, but not from *some* to *all* (§ *79*). Except in quantitative cases, which compare masses, deduction is the determination or specification of a class notion; it descends the logical scale (§ *42*), and thus is *a priori*. It does not generalize, but specifies by inference from intuitions or from inductions.

Inductive inference, on the contrary, by virtue of principles to be presently discussed, ascends the logical scale; it generalizes, proceeding from the particular or the less general to the universal, from *some* to *all*, and thus, in the application of its demonstrated theorems or canons, it is *a posteriori*. The inference from *some* to *all* completes the possible procedures, since every judgment concerns either *all* or *some* of its subject (§ *62*).[1]

dicting axiomatic truth; and it would seem, when the inductive premise expresses a causal relation perfectly ascertained (and the theory presumes perfection), that the induction of a universal follows of necessity, in the sense stated. Hence we have ventured to use this definition as a definition of inference in general, including deductive inference (both immediate and mediate) and inductive inference.

[1] "Induction is inferring a proposition from premises *less general* than itself, and Ratiocination [Deduction] is inferring a proposition from premises *equally* or *more* general."—Mill, *Logic*, p. 125.

It is worth noting that the names Deduction and Induction happily express by their etymology (Lat. *de-ducere* and *in-ducere*) the inverse

This division of the genus inference into deduction and induction, differentiating the latter as a generalization, prepares us for an exact and full definition, thus: **Induction is an immediate synthetic inference generalizing from and beyond experience.**[1]

correlation of the processes. The one is to lead or draw from established generalities new particulars, the other is to lead or draw in unobserved particulars under new generalities. In both the procedure is from the known to the previously unknown.

[1] "Induction is the process from particulars to universals."—Aristotle, *Topica*, i., 12.

"Inductionem enim censemus eam esse demonstrandi formam, quæ sensum tuetur et naturam premit et operibus imminet ac fere immiscetur. . . . At secundum nos, axiomata [propositiones] continentur et gradatim excitantur, ut nonnisi postremo loco ad generalissima veniatur."—Bacon, *Instauratio Magna*, Dist. Op., p. 3.

"Induction is a kind of argument which infers, respecting a whole class, what has been ascertained respecting one or more individuals of that class."—Whately, *Logic*, Index.

Induction is "a formal illation of the universal from the individual, as legitimated solely by the laws of thought, and abstract from the conditions of this or that particular matter."—Hamilton, *Discussions*, p. 157.

"When, having discovered by observation and comparison that certain objects agree in certain respects, we generalize the qualities in which they coincide, that is, when from a certain number of individual instances we infer a general law, we perform what is called an act of Induction."—Hamilton, *Metaphysics*, p. 72.

"Induction is usually defined to be the process of drawing a general law from a sufficient number of particular cases; Deduction is the converse process of proving that some property belongs to a particular case, from the consideration that it comes under a general law."—Thomson, *Outline of the Laws of Thought*, § 113.

"Induction is a term applied to describe the process of a true Colligation of Facts by means of an exact and appropriate Conception."—Whewell, *Novum Organon Renovatum*, bk. ii., aphorism 13.

§ 4. In the definition are collected a number of terms needful to further discriminations. That the inference is immediate will be clearly established in a subsequent discussion (§§ 24, 32).

That the inference is synthetic is evident, since it concludes more than the content of its premise. When from *Some men are mortals*, we infer *All men are mortals*, the subject is augmented, enlarged from the narrow *Some men* of whom we know, to the wide universal *All men;* thus adding to the general class notion something not already contained in it. Besides, the content of the predicate is augmented; for in the premise *Some men are mortals*,

"Induction may be defined, the operation of discovering and proving general propositions."—Mill, *Logic*, p. 208.

"Induction is that operation of the mind by which we infer that what we know to be true in a particular case or cases will be true in all cases which resemble the former in certain assignable respects. In other words, Induction is the process by which we conclude that what is true of certain individuals of a class is true of the whole class, or that what is true at certain times will be true in similar circumstances at all times."—Mill, *Logic*, p. 210.

"Induction may be summarily defined as Generalization from Experience. It consists in inferring from some individual instances in which a phenomenon is observed to occur that it occurs in all instances of a certain class; namely, in all which resemble the former, in what are regarded as the material circumstances."—Mill, *Logic*, p. 223.

"Induction is the generalization of conjoined properties, on the observation of individual instances."—Bain, *Logic*, Int., § 54.

"Induction is the arriving at General Propositions, by means of Observation or fact."—Bain, *Logic*, bk. iii., ch. i., § 1.

In a careful search through Mr. Venn's "Empirical Logic," I was unable to find that he anywhere ventures upon a succinct definition of induction. But see his discussion, ch. xiv.

the class notion *mortals* is only said to contain *some men*, whereas in the conclusion *All men are mortals* the notion *mortals* contains under it *all men*. This adding to both subject and predicate is a double synthesis.

Changing the form from extension to intension (§ *20*) the synthesis remains. From *Some men are mortal*, we infer *All men are mortal.* Here the mark *mortal*, which in the premise is attributed to *some men* only, is in the conclusion attributed to *all men*. The content of the *all men* is thereby enlarged by a synthesis of the mark *mortal;* and the mark itself is synthetically enlarged from its narrow attribution to *some men*, to its wide attribution to *all men.* Thus in this view also we find a double synthesis.[1]

§ 5. The term synthetic in the definition clears induction of a large and important class of judgments which are not synthetic, but analytic. When a predicate belongs to a subject as something which is already though covertly contained in it, the judgment is analytic; as, *Man is an animal, Matter is extended, Birds are oviparous, Table-salt is a chloride.* Such a predicate adds nothing to the conception of the subject, but merely unfolds a constituent mark, essential and original, which is thought already though confusedly in the subject. This

---

[1] There seems to have been a great deal of confusion on this very simple matter. See, for explanations, Hamilton, *Metaphysics*, p. 72; and *Logic*, p. 337. Cf. Venn, *Empirical Logic*, p. 366 sq.

form of predication, then, is analytic, a judgment of partial identity affirming of a subject a portion of its essence.[1]

Moreover, every logical definition, being a full explication of the original and essential marks of the definitum, is an analytic judgment; as, *Man is a rational animal, Matter is extended substance, A bird is a feathered oviparous winged biped, Table-salt is sodium chloride,* also the general definition of Logic, and that of Induction now under discussion. All such judgments being analytic, must be set apart from inductions. Likewise must be set apart all derivatives from analytic judgments; as, *Man is sentient, Matter is divisible, Birds incubate, Table-salt is binary.* These are not inductions. Their generality arises, not from induction, but from the original forming of a class notion and its definition (§§ *16, 35*).

An important consequence of the foregoing distinction is that induction is always and only of logical accidents; for the essence of a subject is attained by its analysis, which essence being predicated yields an analytic judgment. It is often difficult to distinguish between essence and accident, a mark supposed to be the one sometimes turning out on closer inspection to be the other. We may be practically embarrassed by this difficulty; still it is clear, that induction is of accidents only, not of essence.

We have already discriminated deduction from in-

---

[1] A statement of the Kantian distribution of judgments into analytic and synthetic will be found in "The Theory of Thought" (Harper & Bros.), p. 93.

duction; we may take now another view of the distinction. While induction is synthetic, deduction is analytic, since it concludes only a part of the content of its premises. Under *All men are mortals* subsume *All kings are men*, concluding *All kings are mortals*. The conclusion is of narrower generality than the major premise. The process analyzes or resolves the notion *men* into its constituents *kings* and *non-kings*, and concludes concerning the former only. Deduction, therefore, is analytic, and thus is essentially distinct from and logically opposed to induction.

§ 6. The definition limits the inductive inference still further to generalization from experience.

A practical acquaintance with any particular matter by simple observation or by experiment is an experience. Truth thus known is called empirical truth. The generalization of induction, since its ground is experience, is likewise called empirical. But let it be noted that an experience is always and only of a particular individual fact or truth; there is no experience of a general fact or truth, this being a product of thinking. An inference *a posteriori* or from experience is not necessarily true, nor has it independent universality, since it is conditioned on the existing order of things. Moreover, every experience is attended by some uncertainty, for the closest observation of the simplest fact is liable at least to what is called an error of sense, and so far is doubtful. This possibility injects a corresponding uncertainty into the inferred generality. Hence the absence of strict certainty, necessity, and universality is characteristic of empirical knowledge, that derived from experience.[1]

§ 7. To empirical truth evolved by induction is opposed pure truth, that is, truth not derived from experience, but given in intuition.[2] Pure intuitions in the forms of purely intellectual or non-sensuous ideas and principles are characterized by strict certainty, necessity, and universality. Such are the ideas of *space*, of *time*, of *causation*, of *right*; such are the principles or axioms of pure mathematics, as *Two intersecting straight lines cannot enclose an*

---

[1] Empirical, from ἐμπειρία; experience, from *experiri*. Empirical knowledge, the knowledge of experience, is the knowledge that a thing is, γνῶσις ὅτι ἔστι. Speculative or philosophical knowledge, the knowledge of ratiocination, is the knowledge why or how a thing is, γνῶσις διότι ἔστι. See motto on the title-page, taken from Trendelenburg, "Elem. Log. Arist." The distinction, in these terms, is made by Aristotle in many places, e.g., γὰρ τὸ μὲν ὅτι τῶν αἰσθητικῶν εἰδέναι, τὸ δὲ διότι τῶν μαθηματικῶν, etc.—*Anal. Post.*, i. 13. Themistius, his paraphrast, says: διὰ τοῦ σημείου μὲν ὡς τὸ ὅτι, διὰ θατέρου δὲ ὡς τὸ διότι. See Grote, *Aristotle*, ch. vii. p. 322. For empirical, see Hamilton, *Metaphysics*, lec. iii.

[2] Empirical intuitions, and the inferences from them characterizing mediate perceptions, are discussed in my "Elements of Psychology," §§ 87, 96, 157. For pure intuitions, see Id. §§ 113, 124. Also the foot-note in this volume, p. 30. A full consideration of pure truths belongs to philosophy, not to logic. Differing views are held as to their origin and the ground of their undisputed universality. These views do not specially concern us here. Logic needs only to distinguish pure truths from unquestionable inductions, in order to set them, with their direct consequences, clearly apart.

area; also those of logic, as the primary laws (§ 7); also those of ethics, as *Trespass is wrong.* Every rule derived from experience has actual, or possible, or at least conceivable, exceptions; but a rule intuitively discerned by pure reason has universal, unlimited universality, has no exception in all the universe of things. An exception is impossible even in thought.

Let it be remarked that, while pure truth is general in the highest sense, its generality is attained neither by class generalization nor by induction, but by intuition. When upon an empirical occasion such truth is intellectively discerned, it is at once, without any logical process beyond abstraction, seen by the pure intellect or reason to be strictly universal. Hence it is not the result of inductive inference, nor indeed of any kind of inference.

Also we remark that pure principles are synthetic, since the predicate adds something to the subject not already contained in it. But they are not, like inductions, synthetic *a posteriori*, but are synthetic *a priori*, a profound distinction referable to the exercise of pure reason.[1]

---

[1] The phrases *a priori* and *a posteriori* were used by the schoolmen in a sense derived from Aristotle, the former to denote an inference from cause to effect, the latter to denote an inference from effect to cause. More commonly now, in Logic, they are used to distinguish between the deduction of a special from general truth, and the induction of a general truth from observed facts. In Philosophy, knowledge *a priori*, according to Kant, is that which is independent of all experience and logically prior to it; knowledge *a posteriori* is that acquired by observation of facts, and therefore dependent on and logically pos-

By the foregoing criteria pure intuitive truth is distinguished, and should never be confused with the empirical generalities obtained by induction. The importance of this clearance cannot be overestimated. Its difficulty is enhanced by the fact that both pure and empirical truths, though so widely distinct in origin and character, are constantly and intimately connected, and are therefore especially liable to confusion. In the present treatise we shall be largely concerned with both kinds; for logic in general consists essentially of pure truths with deductions from them of formal rules and canons, and incidentally makes application of these to matter, evolving material and empirical truths.[1]

terior to experience. The one is knowledge of pure, the other of empirical, truth. See *Critique of Pure Reason*, Int. § 1; and Hamilton, *Logic*, p. 385 Am. ed.

[1] Sciences which, like Logic, originate in and develop from pure truths or axioms, are strictly demonstrative and exclusively deductive (§ *108*). Thus Inductive Logic is, as to its formal system, deductive. Also let it be noted that Pure Mathematics is exclusively deductive. This is sufficiently obvious, since the formal conclusions it deduces, being already completely general, cannot be further generalized (§ *130*). It does not admit of any inductive inference. Many logicians have maintained the contrary, holding that the law of a series, such as Newton's binomial theorem, is obtained by induction, by generalizing from a few particulars. But upon consideration it will be seen that the law in each case is a deduction from the more general principles of multiplication as applied in permutation and combination. The given members of the series are subsumed, and the law deduced. Besides the already complete generality of all the propositions involved in the process, we point out that the inference to the law is not a synthetic, but an analytic, process. For example, take the simple series 2, 4, 6, 8 - - - - -. Its law is: The nth term $= 2n$. This is discovered by an analysis of the given terms, and adds nothing to what is given.

§ 8. The definition limits the inductive inference finally to generalization beyond experience.

Induction centres in experience, but it makes a circuit of untried regions, and, in accord with the etymology of the word, leads in or brings within its scope a vast assemblage of truths otherwise unknown. It goes far beyond experience, and by synthesis adds unobserved facts to our knowledge, very often ascertaining with scientific accuracy facts that are permanently beyond the reach of possible observation. Moreover, it exhausts the field by its comprehensive *all*. This excursive and inclusive clean sweep is an especial characteristic of induction.

An important consequence of the extension of the inductive inference beyond experience is its liability to include, in the unexplored region, exceptional facts. It is true that in an inductive sequence grounded on thoroughly ascertained causal connection, seeming exceptions must be attributed to unknown counteracting causes, and hence are not truly exceptions. Yet in our ignorance of the possibilities in the outer region, we are not, even in such case, strictly certain, and must admit the notion of possible, or at least conceivable, exceptions. For example, if from observation of many cases it is inferred that *All crows are black*, color being usually considered an unessential mark or accident, it may be objected that albinos have been seen. So also *Every oak-tree bears acorns* is uncertain, for it may be that some are sterile. To the rule *Alkalies have metallic bases* an exception turns up in ammonia. If from finding table-salt, saltpetre, and others, to be soluble I inductively infer *All alkaline salts are soluble*, perhaps no exception could be named; but if I generalize more widely to *All salts are soluble*, my inference is falsified by sulphate of baryta, and many others.

In a previous section (§ 6) an element of uncertainty, due to what are called errors of sense, was pointed out. We now find another, due to generalizing beyond experience. Since exceptions may actually or at least conceivably occur, it follows that the empirical universality attained by induction is to some extent a precarious, a hazardous universality. This hazard is a derived characteristic of induction.

§ 9. A generalization beyond experience is logically opposed to a generalization within experience. Having examined certain individuals of a class, we may sum up our observations in a single general statement. Thus I may know by direct observation, and say of my friends, that *A few are wealthy, Many are prosperous, Most are industrious*. These statements concerning some at least, perhaps all, being partial, are termed approximate generalizations. Thorough observation of each friend may justify my saying, *All are honest, None are covetous*. These statements, being total, are termed complete generalizations, or simply generalizations. In like manner, by an examination of each one separately, I may ascertain that *Every member of my class of pupils is studious*, or that *Each of the apostles was inspired*, or that *All the known planets shine by reflected light*.

Likewise, when it is seen that *A straight line cannot intersect a circle in more than two points*, and that this is true also in case of an ellipse, of a parabola, and of an hyperbola, then, there being no others, we may lay it down as a universal property of conic curves. This last example illustrates the modification that two or more general truths or laws may often be reduced to one comprehensive statement whose extension is no greater than that of its combined components.

This process is truly a generalization, a classification, and of great value in condensing expression; but it is not an induction, for it does not surpass the limits of experience. Yet it has been called an induction, and even a perfect and the only perfect induction.[1] But indeed it is not an inference of any kind, for nothing distinct from what is laid down follows. Evidently it is merely a summation of the known particulars, a colligation of the observed facts, an abridgment of their statement by uniting them under one term. To distinguish it from induction, it may be called a summary or closed generalization, or, more widely, a colligation.

§ 10. We have now explained with illustrations most of the limiting terms in the definition of induc-

---

[1] See the subsequent § 27. "It is in the transition from some observed particulars to the totality of particulars that the real inductive inference consists; not in the transition from the totality to the class-term which denotes that totality, and connotes its determining common attribute."—Grote, *Aristotle*, ch. vi., p. 278.

tion. Also we have indicated and illustrated several forms of thought excluded by those limitations.

Two formal processes, in addition to those already examined, each of which results in a new truth, but neither of which is a generalization, frequently occur, and cause confusion, inasmuch as they are commonly regarded and treated of as inductive processes. For the sake of clearness, it is needful that these also should be here examined, in order to be at once distinguished from induction, and relegated to their rightful places.

One may be illustrated thus: A ship follows an unknown coast. After some days the sailor, having watched the coast and finding himself again at the starting-point, says: *It is an island.* Here is certainly a discovery of a new fact, assigning this land to the familiar sub-class island. Throughout the process there is no generalization whatever; hence it is neither in part nor in whole an induction. Either it is merely a gathering up and piecing together in one the facts of a series of observations, which is only another sort of colligation, one without generalization, or, what is better, it is a discovery of identity establishing a minor premise.

This last phrase requires some explanation. The sailor knows: *A land soon sailed about is an island.* He discovers: *This land is land soon sailed about;* which discovery merely identifies this land with the notion of land soon sailed about, thereby establishing a minor premise, and enabling him to conclude: *This land is an island.* Here is both discovery and deductive proof. No generalization, and therefore no induction, is involved.[1]

In like manner, Kepler, having noted several points in the planet's path, and finding the curve connecting them to be elliptical, determined the orbit of Mars to be an ellipse. It had long been known that this orbit is a curve returning into itself. As a geometer Kepler knew also that a curve returning into itself, with such and such properties, is an ellipse. He identified the orbit of Mars, besides being a curve returning into itself, as having such and such properties. By this identification, he established a minor premise, and concluded the orbit of Mars is an ellipse. Afterward Kepler made the induction, known as his second law, that *All planetary orbits are ellipses*.[2]

Similar instances of enlarged discovery by identification abound. When, after the induction of the laws of magnetism, other metals besides iron, as nickel, cobalt, manganese, chromium, were discovered to be magnetic, the magnetic laws were at once transferred deductively to these metals. Franklin, by use of a kite, identified lightning with electricity. It followed that whatever was inductively true of the one was true of the other.

---

[1] Mr. Mill calls this process a description. See his *Logic*, p. 213 sq., Am. ed.; and the criticism of Dr. Whewell, *Philosophy of Discovery*, ch. xxii., § ii., 15 sq. See also Bain, *Logic*, p. 235 sq., Am. ed.

[2] Kepler's Laws of the Planetary Orbits are as follow:
1st. The radii vectores describe equal areas in equal times.
2d. The orbits are ellipses, with the Sun in one of the foci.
3d. The squares of the periodic times are as the cubes of the mean distances.

Questions of identity to establish a minor premise are necessarily a part of scientific research, but they should not be confused, as they often are, with a precedent process of inductive generalization establishing a major premise or a general law, nor with a subsequent induction to which they may give rise.

§ 11. The other process needing to be distinguished from induction resembles the preceding in being a deduction lying between prior and subsequent inductions; it differs from the preceding in that it is an inquiry, not into identity, but into causal relation. Such investigation involves no generalization, and is often carried on with no present thought of extension beyond the individual case in question.

For example, a coroner's inquest is held to determine the cause of a death. All the immediate circumstances are minutely ascertained, expert medical testimony taken, and all collateral facts set down in detail. Then, subsuming the facts under long-settled and well-known principles and rules, deductions are made, perhaps quite a series, and the cause of the death finally concluded to be this or that. There is no generalization, no induction whatever; and the important fact of the cause in this particular case is ascertained and stated without any intent or thought of extending the conclusion by induction to all similar cases. The procedure indicated is from effect to cause. The reverse may occur. Thus legislators, having fixed a certain tax, watch for its effect upon industry.

The discovery of the planet Neptune by Leverrier and by Adams is a notable example. Perturbations having been observed in the orbital motion of Uranus, each of these astronomers posited hypothetically an exterior planet as the disturbing cause. Then by calculation they assigned the place where finally the telescope revealed its presence. Throughout this process, in order to deduce the result, they used general principles of mathematics, and mechanical and astronomical inductions already established; but they did not make any induction during the process, nor did they, like Kepler, follow it by any inductive generalization.

It is important that the formal procedure here exemplified be clearly and emphatically set apart, especially because, being a necessary preparation for scientific induction, the two are very liable to be confounded, and are actually so confounded by most logical authorities. Preparation for induction is in some cases the observation of only a single fact. For example: *This lodestone attracts this bit of iron.* Now, if the statement be unquestionably true, we may proceed at once to the induction, and say universally: *Lodestone attracts iron.* The example is crude, but even in it we may clearly distinguish the preparatory fact from the subsequent induction.

When the matter is more complex many observations of similar cases may be requisite, accompanied perhaps by much experimental investigation involving numerous deductions, before it is fully established that a certain phenomenon in each of the cases is unquestionably the cause or the effect of another. Then, but not until then, are we properly prepared to make a scientific induction from the experience of these particular cases to all cases of the same class lying beyond experience.

Thus David Wells made many observations, with reasonings therefrom, and many careful experiments on the deposit of dew under various circumstances, before he could justly conclude that this phenomenon in these cases was the effect of a reduction of the temperature of the bedewed surface below a certain point. When this was established, he was then prepared to make the induction of the universal law known as the Wells theory of dew.

The preparation for induction, so far as it involves inference, is deductive, and should not be confused with the subsequent induction. In the progress of the present treatise there will be frequent occasion to remark this distinction.

§ 12. The various distinctions and eliminations proposed in the foregoing sections are all in accord with the stated definition of induction. This will be allowed. But perhaps the definition itself may be questioned. It may be deemed too narrow, or arbitrary, or merely nominal, not real (§ *39*). In reply we can only offer the development of the subject in the following treatise. The definition we have given will, in its numerous and varied applications, be found adequately comprehensive, yet sharply distinctive, of a real mental process of the highest import.

II.—PRINCIPLES

§ 13. It is sufficiently evident that the Primary Laws of Thought cannot be superseded (§ 7 sq.). Their necessity is universal, holding in induction, and throughout its collateral processes. But it is also clear that under these laws alone the inference of *all* from *some* is illicit (§ *79*). Hence this very important inference becomes legitimate only in view of certain principles of similar origin and authority conjoined with the primary laws. Such principles are evolved from the intuitive fact of causation, the root of all induction, and that which gives it validity. They are called the Principles of Induction, or the Laws of Causation, and are applicable to changes or events that are purely physical, and to human affairs.

§ 14. A preliminary examination of the notion of causation is needful. In general, a cause is what determines a change or event. Strictly taken, a change is a ceasing to be; an event, a beginning to be; but we shall use these terms indifferently. The cause determines, without possible alternative, that the event shall be just what it becomes. The cause is antecedent, the event or effect consequent. When the stroke of a hammer breaks a stone, the antecedent blow is the cause, the consequent breaking is the event determined or the effect produced. A cause thus producing an effect is called an efficient cause, to distinguish it from other senses of the word cause which is used commonly and in this treatise without qualification to signify efficient cause.[1]

[1] Aristotle, in "Analyt. Post." II. xi., and "Meta." I. iii., distinguishes four kinds of cause, *αἰτία*, as follow:

1st. The formal cause, τὸ τί ἦν εἶναι, is the form, idea, archetype, or παράδειγμα of a thing. The plan of a building in the mind of the architect is its formal cause.

2d. The material cause, ἡ ὕλη ὑποκειμένη, is the matter subjected to the form. The wood, stone, and iron used in a building constitute its material cause.

3d. The efficient cause, ἡ τί πρῶτον ἐκίνησε, is the proximate mover producing change. The workmen who erect a building are its efficient cause.

4th. The final cause, τὸ τίνος ἕνεκα, is that for the sake of which the thing is done. The purpose or end for which a building is erected is its final cause.

The final cause is prior, he says, in the order of nature, but posterior in the order of time or generation. The efficient cause is prior in time or generation. The formal and the material causes are each simultaneous with its effect, neither prior nor posterior.

But it would, perhaps, be more accurate to say that every cause is simultaneous with its effect. For cause and effect are correlatives—neither can exist without the other; they exist only as they coexist. A cause cannot be so named, except by anticipation, until there is an effect; nor an effect, except by reference to what has already occurred, after the change or event has taken place. Their order of succession is logical, not temporal. *Cessante causâ cessat et effectus* was a scholastic dogma. Mr. Mill speaks doubtfully and rather confusedly.—*Logic*, p. 247 sq. Cf. Hobbes, *Elementa Philosophica*, ch. ix.

The schoolmen made the important subdivision of efficient cause, *causa efficiens*, into the simply genetic *causa essendi*, a cause of being, and *causa cognoscendi*, a cause of knowing, a reason (§ *110*). Aristotle uses *αἰτία* in this latter sense even when treating of induction,

A condition, in general, is an antecedent that must be in order that something else may be. A causal condition is, specifically, an antecedent determining the event (§ *110*). A merely temporal antecedent is followed by a subsequent; a causal antecedent by a consequent. Mere succession in time, however invariable, does not imply causation. Night is followed by day, but is not its cause. Day is not conditioned on night, but on a rising sun, and this, then, is the cause of day, or its determining condition. There may be a quasi-sequence in time, as when inoculation is followed by small-pox; or none, as when by expenditure of energy a cannon-ball instantly shatters a wall.

§ 15. In the foregoing example of a hammer and a stone a single antecedent is named as the cause, and single consequent as the effect. This is the usage of common speech. Such a selection from several antecedents or consequents of some one as the cause or the effect is often quite arbitrary. When a stone falls to the ground, the cause may be said to be the earth, or gravity, or the weight of the stone, or the stone itself. We may say the explosion destroyed the magazine, or that it shook the land, or was heard miles away. The selection is perhaps influenced by concomitant thoughts, or determined by some special

ἐπαγωγή, in "Analyt. Prior," II., xxiii., which has occasioned much confusion in the views of his interpreters. In the present treatise the unqualified word *cause* must be understood to mean, as it does in modern usage, *causa efficiens essendi*.

interest. Most frequently that antecedent which, added to those already assembled, completes the collocation requisite to produce the change is called the cause; as, *A spark caused the explosion;* or, *An east wind produced the rain;* or, *Malaria induced the fever.* But it is evident that in these cases, and likewise in all cases, neither the cause nor the effect is single and simple. There must be a conjunction of at least two things to produce a change in either, and both are thereby changed. There is always more than one causal condition or antecedent, and more than one determined consequent.

Even a purely negative fact is often spoken of as a cause; as, *The cakes were burned because of Alfred's inattention.* Obviously this is unscientific. More properly the thought is that an event occurred when a preventing cause was withdrawn. The phrase, preventing cause, is a convenient designation of any member of a given collocation of antecedents whose presence hinders change; as in the examples: *A friction match does not ignite because it is wet; A scotched wheel does not revolve; An anæsthetic prevents pain; an antiseptic, decay.* But the notion of a preventive cause is negative, and inaccurate, for in strictness a cause is essentially positive.

§ 16. In seeking, then, a full knowledge of the cause or the effect of a phenomenon, all positive circumstances are to be inspected; and, having eliminated those that are immaterial, *i. e.*, not concerned in the case, we enumerate the rest, recognizing as the cause all conditioning antecedents, and as the effect all conditioned consequents, and omitting to state only those that are quite obvious. For instance, a cause is a hammer in motion and a whole stone; its effect, a hammer at rest and a broken stone.¹ It may be very difficult or even quite impracticable to enumerate completely the antecedents concerned in producing an effect, or the consequents of their interaction, but nothing short of this can be accepted as entire theoretical accuracy, though, indeed, all inductive sciences have to be content with merely approximate statements. Thus, popularly speaking, the cause of vision is light entering the eye; but a scientific statement would include the optical action of the lenses of the eye, the physiology of its coats, and of the nerves and brain, together with the connection between a special activity of the brain and a state of mind, a sense-perception. Still the enumeration would be only approximate. To state even approximately the effect in vision would require a much more subtle analysis. The theoretic ideal re-

---

[1] The notion of cause and effect is confused in many minds with the notion of agent and patient, whereas the two notions are very different. The latter distinction, that of agent and patient, occurs only among the antecedents or causes of an event; as, the hammer strikes, the stone is struck. The manifestly active member is regarded as the agent, the apparently quiescent member as the recipient or patient affected. Still this is arbitrary. We may say, the stone resists, the hammer is resisted. The distinction, except when referable to Will as a determining antecedent, depends merely on the point of view, and hence, though often convenient, is unessential. See Mill, *Logic*, p. 242.

quires an exhaustive statement, towards which ideal our practice strives.

These considerations explain and will justify the following correlative definitions:

A cause is the aggregate of all the positively conditioning antecedents of an event.

An effect is the aggregate of all the positively conditioned consequents in an event.[1]

§ 17. In the notion of a cause as an efficient agent is implied the notion of a force producing the effect, and this force is properly and scientifically regarded as the cause. The aggregate of the antecedents is the source of the force, or, more strictly, the force is manifested by an aggregate of antecedents of which it is the property or function. Examples are, gravity, cohesion, muscular effort, etc.

Recent physics, while it regards force as the ever-present agent of physical change, represents all physical changes or events as consisting in a transferring with often a transforming of energy. Some of the

---

[1] Mr. Mill's definition of cause has been widely discussed and approved. He says: "The cause of a phenomenon is the antecedent, or the concurrence of antecedents, on which it is invariably and unconditionally consequent."—*Logic*, p. 245. Mr. Venn says: "This view of causation is very generally accepted in science and in the logical treatises on Inductive Philosophy, if indeed it may not be termed the popular view." He then makes some critical remarks.— *Logic of Chance*, ch. ix. We have ventured to propose a modified statement, because the important terms *invariably* and *unconditionally* are negative, and because the former superfluously implies uniformity (§ 19). Cf. Hobbes, *Elementa Philosophica*, ch. ix.

principal forms of energy which are capable of mutual transformation are mechanical, thermal (heat and light), electrical, chemical, and neural energy.

It has been proved in many cases, by accurate measurements of the work done within a given system or aggregate of things, that the quantity of energy therein transferred or transformed or both is constant. There is neither gain nor loss. Hence it is inductively inferred that, while in the internal changes of a group there may be alteration in the forms of energy, there is no alteration of its quantity. This is the Law of Conservation of Energy (§ 98 n.). It affirms that, just as the quantity of matter in the universe is unalterable, so the quantity of energy is unalterable; though, indeed, these statements are identical, matter being known only by the manifestation of energy.

The law of conservation is supplemented by the important distinction between kinetic or actual and potential energy. In gunpowder is stored up a vast amount of potential energy which is set free or becomes kinetic by virtue of the kinetic energy of a spark. It is the sum of the kinetic and potential energies that is constant, while in almost every change there is a passing more or less complete of one into the other.

In this modified and refined view we define thus:

Causation is the transfer, with more or less transformation, of a definite amount of energy, measured by the amount of work done, and effecting a new distribution.

Physical science of to-day is largely occupied with the measurement of passing energy in various cases, with the determination of the quantity rather than the kind of causes and their correlative effects. But in all of these investigations, under modified doctrines and varied terminology, the logical processes are formally identical, and there is no need to alter the view of causation presented in the previous sections in order to unfold the fundamental processes of thought involved in physical research.

§ 18. It has already been said that from the intuitive fact of causation are evolved the special Principles of Induction, or Laws of Causation (§ 13). They are primarily two, the first in logical order being the PRINCIPLE or AXIOM of CHANGE, as follows:

Every change (or event) has a cause.

This axiom, by virtue of its predominating pure element, causation, has philosophical necessity (§ 5), and is strictly universal (§ 7). The bare possibility of a single exception is utterly inconceivable.[1] There lurks an essential self-contradiction in the phrase, *An uncaused event* (§ 9). The word *chance*, when used in that sense, has no meaning whatever; there is no possible notion, and no possible fact cor-

---

[1] The principle is intuitively true, though not altogether pure. The notion of cause is strictly pure, but the notion of change (or event) is empirical—that is, it can be had only from experience. See Kant, *C. P. R.*, Int., § 1. Change, referred to the consciousness of the observer, is the very essence of experience, and is the occasion of the pure intellectual intuition of causation. See *Psychology*, §§ 114, 126.

responding to it (§ 48). Whenever any change is experienced, the pure intellect or reason intuitively discerns that it must have a cause, an efficient determining cause.¹ What is the cause may be in most cases very questionable, but that there is a determining cause in each and every case is strictly unquestionable, or rather is clearly and truly discernible. The axiom is not merely a law of thought, but is also a law of things, not merely a logical subjective necessity, but a real objective necessity in nature,

[1] This doctrine of the origin of the present and of other axioms is according to the intuitional philosophy. The opposed empirical philosophy teaches that all axioms are themselves inductions from experience, inductions of widest and unexceptional generality. The question is discussed in my "Elements of Psychology," § 124 sq. See also above, § 7, and below, § 19 note. Dr. Whewell in his "Philosophy of Discovery," ch. xxii., severely criticises Mr. Mill's "Logic," and in § 71 very aptly says that axioms "may be much better described as conditions of experience than as results of experience." For illustration of our view: *A whole is equal to the sum of its parts* is the axiomatic basis of chemical quantitative analysis; but should we make an induction from the myriads of analyses that have been published, the inference would be: *A whole is never equal to, but ever less than, the sum of its parts.*

But as already observed, § 7, note, the question of the origin of axioms is philosophical, not logical. It might be entirely disregarded in this treatise, since all logicians, empiricists as well as intuitionists, accept them as irrefragable and unexceptionable, and therefore a safe and sufficient basis of logical doctrine and scientific proof.

Let us, however, instance their catholicity. So firm is the deep though obscure conviction in every mind that *Every change is caused*, that when a change (event) occurs with no assignable causal antecedents, men are prone to invent a cause, a groundless hypothesis; and so it comes that in ignorance, in the absence of any apparent natural cause, one supernatural is often posited; hence false spiritualism, and, in general, superstition.

holding true throughout the universe, in all space everywhere, in all time, past, present, and future.[1]

The axiom may be stated: *If change is, cause is;* hence (§ *119*), *If cause is not, change is not.* This form is illustrated by the first law of motion, which affirms that a body in motion, if not acted on by some disturbing cause, will continue to move with uniform velocity and in the same direction forever.[2]

§ 19. The second of the two Laws of Causation is the PRINCIPLE or AXIOM of UNIFORMITY. It is subdivided into two axioms, the first of which is as follows:

Like causes have like effects.[3]

The word *like* here is to be very strictly construed. It means more than general resemblance, or striking

---

[1] Burgersdyck says very neatly: *Quicquid fit ab alio fit, nihil fit a seipso.*

[2] Newton's Three Laws of Motion, "Principia," Introduction, are as follow:

1st. Every body perseveres in its state of rest, or of uniform motion in a right line, unless it is compelled to change its state by forces impressed upon it.

2d. Change of motion is proportional to the motive force impressed, and is made in the right line in which that force is impressed.

3d. Reaction is always contrary and equal to action; or, the actions of two bodies upon each other are always equal, and directed to contrary parts.

[3] It might be very correctly stated: Like causes produce, or determine, or enforce, like effects. But it is needless for logical purposes to insist on the bond of efficiency. Mr. Mill, following the doctrine of Hume, and in entire consistency with his own empirical philosophy, says: "The notion of causation is deemed, by the schools of metaphysics most in vogue at the present moment, to imply a mysterious

similarity. It is not merely that observation, even the most skilful and minute, cannot distinguish certain cases by any other particular than place or time,

and most powerful tie, such as cannot, or at least does not, exist between any physical fact and that other physical fact on which it is invariably consequent, and which is popularly termed its cause; and thence is deduced the supposed necessity of ascending higher, into the essence and inherent constitution of things, to find the true cause, the cause which is not only followed by, but actually produces, the effect. No such necessity exists for the purposes of the present inquiry, nor will any such doctrine be found in the following pages."—*Logic*, p. 236. Nevertheless he frequently speaks of causes as producing their effects, and uses the word *force* a hundred times "in the following pages." How could he do otherwise, while, apart from metaphysics, recent physics is almost wholly occupied with the doctrines of force and energy? Again, he says: "The causes with which I concern myself are not *efficient*, but physical causes."—*Ibid.* Why then should he ever use the word *effect?*

Mr. Mill posits this first Axiom of Uniformity as the "Ground of Induction."—*Logic*, title of ch. iii., bk. iii. In the first section of the chapter (p. 225) he says: "I regard it as itself a generalization from experience." That is to say: Induction is grounded on the axiom of uniformity, and the axiom of uniformity is grounded on induction. This vicious circle he labors, in ch. xxi., with all his great acumen, to justify, and finds in simple enumeration, avowedly the weakest form of induction, which "in science carries us but a little way," the source and strength of the ultimate Axiom of Uniformity. See below, § 40, note. This remarkable attitude of the eminent logician is a necessary consequence of his underlying philosophy, and is a suicidal *reductio ad absurdum* of empiricism.

It is with much hesitation and sincere regret that these points are noted. Such is my high esteem of Mr. Mill as an acute, comprehensive, and profound thinker, that I do not differ from him when I can help it. Happily the exceptions taken relate to his philosophical principle, rather than to his logical doctrine, and do not materially affect the latter. The world of science is profoundly indebted to him for the clearest exposition that has been made since Aristotle of its logical methods. Bacon pointed out the way, Mill laid it open.

but that the cases really and strictly do not at all differ in any other particular.¹

It is evident, upon clear reflection, that this axiom has the same origin and character as the axiom of change; that, when rigidly construed, it is necessarily and universally true, without possible exception in nature or in thought.

§ 20. It very often happens, however, that various phenomena are due to indistinguishable causes. A certain medicine in one case cures, in another kills. A chemist in one case obtains crystals of a salt from its solution, in another he fails. Clouds apparently alike emit at one time lightning, at another rain, at another hail, at another snow. Heat softens iron and hardens clay, it warms to life and scorches to death, it causes chemical composition and decomposition, it melts ice, then contracts the water, then expands it, then turns it to vapor. Electricity is likewise supposed to do of itself a great variety of things.

This mode of statement arises from imperfect observation, or from an interest that assigns to some single antecedent a predominance, as though it alone were the cause (§ 15). In every such instance, however, there is an incomplete estimate of the causal

---

¹ It should be remarked that the word *like* or *similar* is sometimes replaced by the word *same*, this word being often used to express, not strict identity, but the close similarity in things that are distinguishable only numerically, only by place or time. Place and time are real conditions, but not causal conditions, of an event (§ *110*), and hence are not to be reckoned among its causal antecedents.

conditions, and every clear-thinking scientist knows, with a strict certainty admitting of no hesitation or question, that any variation whatever in the consequents is due to some difference in the antecedents, though he be unable to discern or demonstrate any difference. This he knows by virtue of the principle of uniformity. Even the careless observer of ordinary events regulates his thoughts and actions, though obscurely and confusedly, by the same principle.

Yet, as a concession to an interest, or more frequently to a specific ignorance incident to the practical impossibility of making a complete analysis and estimate of the antecedents, a doctrine of so-called Plurality of Effects is allowed, as expressed in the MAXIM: *Regard indistinguishable causes as having apparently a variety of effects.*

Every substance has a variety of properties, and substances are distinguished from each other by their different properties. A property is the capability of a body to produce a specific effect. Every body, then, is a cause producing, according to the foregoing maxim, a variety of effects. Thus the sun deflects the course of the planets, and emits light and heat, because of its attractive, luminiferous, and calorific properties. The earth has attractive and magnetic properties. Steel is hard, heavy, lustrous, and elastic. But it is evident that no body manifests a property except in combination with some other thing. Its color, for example, becomes manifest only in its combination with light and vision. This class of cases, then, does not differ from that already described. Different antecedents only are followed by different consequents. Whenever all the causal antecedents are alike, the consequents are alike.

Again, it is usual to speak of different or even opposed phenomena, when invariably coexistent, as the effects of a common cause. Since doubly refracting substances always exhibit periodical colors on exposure to polarized light, these diverse phenomena have been attributed to a hypothetical common cause. The aurora is invariably accompanied by magnetic disturbance, hence doubtless a common though unknown cause. There is a simultaneous rise of tides on opposite sides of the earth, of which phenomena the moon is known to be the common cause. Such joint effects, whether in the same or in different degrees of descent from the cause, are said to be causally connected, or related through some fact of causation. This mode of representation is convenient, and in accord with the maxim. But the axiom holds good; for the common cause of different phenomena invariably coexistent means only that amidst their distinctly various antecedents some one at least is common.

§ 21. The second axiom of uniformity reverses the first, and is its complement, as follows:

Like effects have like causes.

The same strict construction is to be put on the terms of this axiom as on those of its fellow. It has the same intuitive origin, the same necessary and universal character. That it is an axiom at all has rarely if ever been recognized by logicians of any school. Yet many of the refinements of recent science not only proceed upon it, but would be impossible without it, and it is high time it should take its place in logic. For when all the antecedents and all the consequents are taken into account, either of these groups equally and absolutely implies the other. From a complete knowledge of one the other may infallibly be inferred. Logically, the past is just as truly contained in its future as the future in its past.[1]

[1] The second axiom of uniformity is formally involved in Newton's famous "Regulæ Philosophandi," introducing bk. iii. of the "Principia." The first two of the four Rules, with his comments, are:

1st. No more causes of natural things should be admitted than such as are both true (*veræ*) and sufficient to explain their phenomena.

Accordingly philosophers say: Nature does nothing in vain, and it is vain to do by many what can be done by fewer. For nature is simple, and does not luxuriate in superfluous causes of things.

2d. And therefore (*ideoque*) of natural effects of the same kind the same causes are to be assigned, as far as possible (*quatenus fieri potest*).

As, respiration in man and in beast; descent of stones in Europe and in America; light in culinary fire and in the sun; reflection of light in the earth and in the planets.

To these comments of Newton we venture to add the remark that the illation (*ideoque*) of the second rule from the first is to be construed, not as a deduction, but as an implication. See § 78, and "Theory of Thought," p. 103. Also we remark that both rules are likewise implied in the Law of Parcimony, sometimes called Occam's razor, to which Newton probably had reference in his first comment. See *Psychology*, § 83, note. Also Aristotle says: ὁ θεὸς καὶ ἡ φύσις οὐδὲν μάτην ποιοῦσιν.—*De Cælo*, i., 4. Dr. Whewell, in "Philosophy of Discovery," ch. xviii., § 5 sq., descants at some length on these rules.

By virtue of the axiom implied in the rules, that like effects have like causes, Newton identified celestial with terrestrial gravity. Indeed, he laid down the Rules in anticipation and justification of the proof which follows in bk. iii. Also Franklin's identification of light-

§ 22. It very often happens, however, that various phenomena give rise to indistinguishable effects. Our powers of observation, even when highly skilled and aided by the best microscopes and instruments of precision, are very limited, and in general can distinguish only the grosser elements of causes or of effects. Hence it is rarely possible to pronounce two events strictly alike. Moreover, from the grosser elements of an effect, some one is usually selected, because of its special interest, and treated as though it alone were the effect, all other consequents being disregarded. These considerations explain the practice, even in scientific treatises, of viewing similar effects as the products of dissimilar causes. It is clearly a fiction, and in strictness an impossibility. Yet, in concession to this mode of speech, which is convenient and advantageous when not misleading, a doctrine of so-called Plurality of Causes is admitted, as expressed in the MAXIM: *Regard indistinguishable effects as having apparently a variety of causes.*

Accordingly it is allowed that a man's death is

---

ning with electricity is by virtue of this axiom. Also the Law of the Conservation of Energy finds its basis therein (§ 17).

But illustrations from physical science are needless when we consider that our sensations are effects by which we identify or recognize substances which affect us by their properties. How do I recognize my friend? The like effect on me of a presence I attribute to a like cause. I identify a given substance as gold, only because its effect on me is like to that produced by gold. I distinguish gold and silver by their unlike effects. It is clear, then, that this axiom lies in the very foundation of all knowledge. See, on Genesis of Mediate Perceptions, *Psychology*, §§ 158, 159.

caused in one case by a bullet entering the brain, in another by a knife cutting the heart, in another by a fever ravaging the intestines, and so on, it being impossible to enumerate the various causes of death. There is no objection to such expressions, if we are not misled by them. Let it be noted that death is a purely negative and abstract notion, whereas we are dealing with positive and concrete phenomena. In the first case cited, the causal antecedents are a man and an entering bullet; the effected consequents are a corpse and a torn brain; and so on. It is evident, even in this gross view, that any variation in a total cause gives rise to a variation in its total effect. We allow the useful fiction of a plurality of causes, but hold, in strict construction, to rigid invariability, to uniformity.

Another standard example is heat. It is produced by combustion, by friction, by compression, by electricity, etc. It would be easy to show that heat also is only one fact in an aggregate of consequents varying in each case. But it is better, perhaps, to say that in each case there is a transfer of energy, effecting a new distribution, partly in the form of heat (§ 17). As to the sense-perception of heat, or of white, there is some one condition or set of conditions which is present in every case, and whose presence always produces in us that sense-perception.[1]

---

[1] For the usual view of the doctrine of Plurality of Causes, not recognizing the second axiom of uniformity, see Mill, *Logic*, bk. iii., ch. x.; followed by Bain, bk. iii., ch. viii. Mr. Venn's view is not unlike that of our text. See his *Empirical Logic*, pp. 62, 88. On

Another example, one not so readily reduced, is from the composition of motion. If a ball receive two simultaneous impacts differing in direction and intensity, motion is imparted to it, manifest by its passing along a certain line with a certain velocity. Now the number of impacts which will produce precisely this effect, also their possible variations in direction, or in intensity, is infinite. Here, then, it seems we have an infinite plurality of causes determining an identical effect; for, by the second law of motion, a universal law of nature, the resultant in all cases must be the same.[1] This appears to be a demonstration of plurality of causes; that its maxim is rather a principle, falsifying the second axiom of uniformity. But the resultant motion of the ball is only one fact among others, the only one patent to observation perhaps, but not standing alone. Could we estimate the stress of each impact on the ball, and the consequence to its interior, together with the arrest of the impelling agents, evidently we should find that the aggregate of consequents varies with every variation in the cause.

§ 23. The two axioms of uniformity express all that is properly meant by the familiar phrase: *Uniformity of Nature*, which is sometimes more widely

---

page 421 he says: "The doctrine of Plurality of Causes is a prominent one in Mill's scheme, and he even attaches too great importance to it by regarding the plurality rather as formulated by nature than as arising merely out of practical convenience and convention."

[1] Newton's Corollary I, from the Laws of Motion. See p. 31, note.

and thereby erroneously construed.¹ They clearly hold good in theoretical strictness, and should regulate observation and inference "as far as possible."² The maxims of plurality are practically admissible only as a guard against errors arising from defective or interested observation. In this respect they render important service, especially in those ordinary concerns of life wherein only some part of a cause or of an effect needs consideration.

When the axioms of uniformity are compared, it will be seen that each might be stated more fully, thus: *Only like causes have like effects*, and *Only like effects have like causes*. The first of these compound statements implies: *Unlike causes have unlike effects;* the second implies: *Unlike effects have unlike causes* (§ *71*). Hence, also, if either is, the other is; and if either is not, the other is not; the form being *conditio sine qua non* (§ *119*).

---

[1] The phrase obviously requires limitation. No two leaves of the forest are alike, no two human faces are alike, one star differeth from another star in glory. So far from being uniform, unanalyzed nature presents an infinite variety. Likewise, the statement that the course of nature is uniform, taken in an unlimited sense, is not true. The events of each day are unlike those of any previous day, and no one expects history to repeat itself. But amidst this infinite variety, we discern certain uniformities conforming to the principle that like causes have like effects, and the reverse, which uniformities reduced to general expression are termed laws. In this very important sense, but in no other, is the constitution and course of nature uniform.

[2] This phrase in the second Rule, § 21, note, seems to refer to the very general impracticability of making an exhaustive estimate of the causal conditions of a given effect.

III.—PROCESS

§ 24. Sitting by my anthracite fire, I thrust the poker between the bars of the grate, and after a while, on drawing it out, see that it is red-hot; it shines in the dark. A pyrometer at hand shows that it has reached 1000° F. Here is an experience, specifically an observation by trial or experiment, with quantitative measurement. The result is: *This body of iron heated to* 1000° *F. has become luminous or glows.* It states a particular, individual fact respecting this piece of iron at this time and place, and in the present circumstances.

Then from this single fact I infer immediately the universal proposition: *Any and every body of iron, at any time and any where, heated to* 1000° *F., becomes self-luminous.* This immediate inference is an induction.

§ 25. Let us note, in the first place, that the foregoing inference conforms strictly to other terms in the definition of induction (§ 3). It is synthetic, since the predicate adds to the general notion *body of iron*, something not already contained in it. It obviously generalizes both from experience and beyond experience. The basis from which it proceeds is my experimental observation of a fact. It surpasses all experience by bringing in or inducting under a universal statement every strictly similar fact occurring anywhere in the earth, in the planets, in the stellar spaces, at any time in the unlimited past, present, or future.[1]

Secondly, it is in accord with the principle or axiom of change (§ 18). A change is observed in the iron from dull cold to bright hot. By the axiom, there must be a cause for this changed state in which we take an especial interest. We observe the aggregate of the positively conditioning antecedents, finding it, in the rough, to be burning coal and dull cold iron. This, then, is the cause, having for its consequents burnt coal and bright hot iron, the aggregate effect (§ 16). A more refined view regards the aggregate of antecedents as the present source of a force or cause, determining, in this case, a transfer to the iron of thermal energy of sufficient intensity to affect vision (§ 17).

The causal relation being experimentally and definitely ascertained, we note, thirdly, that the inference conforms to the first axiom of uniformity (§ 19). It assumes that like causes may occur or have occurred at other times and places, and concludes that in all

---

[1] The notion, not infrequent, that induction bears some special relation to the future, needs correction. Time, in its modifications of present, past, and future, is not an element in the inference; nor is place, near or remote. We do not infer from now to then, nor from here to there, but from facts observed to facts unobserved, regardless of time or place. See p. 33, note. On time in judgment see § 60.

such cases like effects must follow. This inductive step is fully authorized by the axiom. The axiom itself is merely and strictly formal; the material case conforms to it, and so is justified. It should be remarked, however, that there is a varying degree of hazard in drawing the conclusion, arising not from the principles involved, but from the uncertainty, always greater or less, respecting the observed facts and their causal relation, no empirical matter ever attaining the strict certainty of intuitive truth (§ 8). In the example, the quantity and shape of the iron are disregarded, being considered immaterial circumstances; but, this one experiment being taken as the sole ground, it might fairly be questioned whether the like effect would follow in a spherical ton of iron, and so further experiments be prerequisite to the general conclusion.

§ 26. In examining the inductive process, it is very important to observe that the inference is immediate. This is true of every proper induction. There is no middle term, one cannot be, for both terms of the conclusion occur in the same premise; hence, no syllogism; the step is strictly and exclusively immediate.

Having established the causal relation between a phenomenon and some circumstance, we proceed, in conformity with one or the other of the axioms. One of the axioms is: *Like causes have like effects.* The corresponding formula is simply as follows:

> In this case A causes a ;
> ∴ In all cases A causes a.

The other axiom is: *Like effects have like causes.* The corresponding formula is simply as follows:

In this case a is the effect of A;
∴ In all cases a is the effect of A.

The inductive process herein formulated needs to be especially remarked, explained, justified, and emphasized; not only because its immediacy is an invariable characteristic, but also because many eminent logicians and their disciples are at fault on this important point, holding that induction is essentially a mediate process, and reducible to the formal syllogism. It seems hard to avoid confusing the inductive inference and other inferences often associated with it, and to see clearly that it is simple, plain, direct, and immediate.[1]

§ 27. It is usual to quote Aristotle in support of the view that the inductive process is a mediate inference, a syllogism. He has the following form:

X, Y, Z are B;
X, Y, Z are all A;
∴ All A are B.

This he calls a syllogism, using the word generically,

---

[1] Dr. Whewell's view is not clear, but it seems consonant with our own on this point. He says: "The process of induction includes a mysterious step, by which we pass from particulars to generals, of which step the reason always seems to be inadequately rendered by any words we can use; and this step to most minds is not demonstrative, as to few is it given to perform it on a great scale."—*Philosophy of Discovery*, ch. xxii., § 66.

in its etymological sense; specifically, a rhetorical syllogism.¹ In the same passage he says induction is contrary to syllogism, meaning logical syllogism. That the form is not a logical syllogism is evident; for the second proposition is one of entire identity; there are, then, but two terms in all; and hence the question is begged (§ *146*). Aristotle's example is:

> Man, horse, mule, etc., are long-lived;
> Man, horse, mule, etc., are acholous (or Γ);
> ∴ All acholous (or Γ) animals are long-lived.

He adds: We must conceive that Γ consists of a collection of all the particular cases. This, he says, is induction. His followers, and many logicians of to-day, call it a perfect, and the only perfect, induction. But the process is from *all* to *all;* and that ambiguously, the first *all* being cumular, the second distributive (§§ *64, 74*). Moreover, not generalizing beyond experience, the process is a closed generalization, a mere summary, a colligation, and therefore not at all an induction in the modern or Baconian sense (§ 9). Aristotle nowhere treats of induction in the latter sense. It was reserved for Bacon to found this complementary branch of logic.²

---

¹ Syllogism, συν-λέγειν, to collect together; like conclusion, *con-cludere*, to shut up together.—*Theory of Thought*, p. 130. Aristotle speaks of a conclusion as "a perfect syllogism of the extremes." The above form he calls ὁ ἐξ ἐπαγωγῆς συλλογισμός.—*Prior Analyt.*, ii., 23. For the word ἐπᾰγωγή (ἐπι-ἄγειν, to lead or bring upon), see Thomson, *Outline, etc.*, § 113, note. It means here an accumulation, a summation, a colligation (§ 9). Cicero, "De Inv.," fairly translates it by *inductio*, but it is quite different from the modern induction.

² Aristotle says distinctly: We believe everything either through

§ 28.
Another syllogistic form, laid down as that of the mediate process essential in all induction, is exemplified thus:

This, that, and the other magnet attract iron,
This, that, and the other magnet represent all magnets;
∴ All magnets attract iron.[1]

The correct conclusion in *Darapti* as authorized by the premises is the following:

∴ Some things that represent all magnets attract iron.

---

syllogism or from induction—ἅπαντα γὰρ πιστεύομεν ἢ διὰ συλλογισμοῦ ἢ ἐξ ἐπαγωγῆς.—*Prior Analyt.*, ii., 23. Here as well as in other passages he notes the two processes as entirely distinct. But he forgets or relinquishes this, when he presents to us, in the same chapter, the inductive process as a variety of the syllogism. His view has been much discussed. Dr. Whewell, "Phil. of Disc.," Appendix D, examines it at length, and concludes: "Induction from a comparatively small number of particular cases to a general law stands in opposition to the syllogism. . . . Induction is inconclusive as reasoning. It is not reasoning; it is another way of getting at truth. . . . As true inductive propositions cannot be logically demonstrated by syllogistic rules, so they cannot be discovered by any rule." Mr. Grote, "Aristotle," ch. vi., p. 268 sq., also discusses the matter at length, and concludes: "We thus see that this very peculiar syllogism is (as indeed Aristotle himself remarks) the opposite or antithesis of a genuine syllogism. It has no proper middle term; the conclusion in which it results is [identical with] the first or major proposition, the characteristic feature of which it is to be *immediate*, or not demonstrated through a middle term" (p. 273). . . . "These chapters respecting induction and example are among the most obscure and perplexing in the Aristotelian Analytica. The attempt to throw both into the syllogistic form is alike complicated and unfortunate; moreover, the reasoning has hitherto been imperfectly apprehended" (p. 275).

[1] This form is given by Hamilton in his "Metaphysics," p. 72; and more fully developed and defended in his "Logic," § lxii. See also his *Discussions*, p. 156 sq.

But this is not at all what is proposed to be proved. The conclusion sought and stated is not syllogistically authorized, the term *all magnets* not occurring in either premise; and hence that conclusion is irrelevant (§ *144*). We remark, however, that the given form, though not a true syllogism of any kind, yet involves an immediate inductive inference from the first premise directly to the conclusion. The intermediate proposition is superfluous, being merely a statement in concrete terms of the axiom of uniformity authorizing the induction of *all*. Its omission does not reduce the form to an enthymeme, for not this material proposition, but only the formal axiom, is in mind.

§ 29. Very eminent authorities unite in proposing the following as a type of the inductive syllogism:

Whatever is true of John, Peter, etc., is true of all mankind;
Mortality is true of John, Peter, etc.;
∴ Mortality is true of all mankind.[1]

---

[1] This form is given by Whately in his "Logic," bk. iv., ch. i., § 1. It i quoted and approved by Mill, "Logic," p. 225. On the previous page he says: "As Whately remarks, every induction is a syllogism with the major premise suppressed; or (as I prefer expressing it) every induction may be thrown into the form of a syllogism, by supplying a major premise." On this Grote comments thus: "Even with this modified phraseology, I cannot admit the propriety of throwing Induction into syllogistic forms of argument. By doing this we efface the special character of Induction, as the jump from particular cases, more or fewer, to an universal proposition comprising them and an indefinite number of others besides. To state this in forms which

This truly is a syllogism. But is it an induction? Not at all. The inference is not from *some* to *all.* The first proposition, whose pre-designation is *Whatever*, is by far the widest of the three, and the deduction from it is a faultless *Barbara*. But, say its advocates, the major premise is an induction; meaning that it is obtained by induction. Granted; but that does not affect the character of the inference before us, which is undeniably a strictly deductive syllogism, proceeding from the more to the less general. When we ask these advocates: How do you get this major, their reply is, that it is the conclusion of a prior and wider syllogism, whose major premise is obtained in like manner, and so on, until we reach the axiom of uniformity, which is the ultimate or primary major premise of the series.[1] That is to say, induction is deduction from the axiom of uniformity.

§ 30. To the doctrine that induction is a mediate procedure from an axiomatic premise, we object:

First, the doctrine is confusing. It denies any specific difference between the processes of deduction and induction. That they are supposed to arise

imply that it is a necessary step, involving nothing more than the interpretation of a higher universal proposition, appears to me unphilosophical."—*Aristotle*, ch. vi., p. 280.

It is curious to note that Mr. Mill, our highest authority in Logic, holds: 1st. That a syllogism does not and cannot prove anything; 2d. That induction alone is proof; 3d. That induction proceeds by syllogism. In his *Logic*, cf. bk. ii., ch. 3, with bk. iii., chs. 1 and 3.

[1] Mill, *Logic*, p. 225.

from different ultimate premises, their several axioms, is not a logical difference, and does not justify that distinction of the methods warmly insisted on by the advocates of this view, and conventionally established and recognized as the Aristotelian and Baconian methods.

Secondly, it is unnatural. Logic is in no respect an invention, but only a distinct statement of the principles and a development of the formal processes by which the human intellect actually discovers and establishes truth, whether of commonplace matter or of recondite science (§ *3*). Now, does the vulgar or the child mind come to know that *Water quenches fire* by a deduction, through a series of syllogisms, from the principle of uniformity as a primary major premise? It would give the skilled sophist some trouble to construct the series, if it be practicable at all; and the supposition that ignorant and stupid people, to whom this and like truths are perfectly well known, have acquired the knowledge by an intricate syllogistic process, however obscurely performed, is incredible.

Thirdly, it is unnecessary. The doctrine may be replaced by one much simpler, which substitute will be confirmed by a little introspection. As the humblest intellect knows, obscurely it may be, yet with a clearness sufficient for practical application, that *Part of a part is part of the whole* (§§ *93, 131*), and thereby is able to appreciate the cogency of a simple syllogism conformed to this formula, so it knows, with similar obscurity perhaps, that *Like causes have like effects*, and a single observation of water quenching fire suffices to establish the general conclusion immediately drawn according to this formula.

Fourthly, it is not true, which is shown in the section following.

§ 31. Let us remark, more particularly than heretofore (§ 2), upon the function of a form. Turning to Pure Mathematics, a science of forms, we note such familiar instances as $1:2=3:6$; $(x+y)(x-y)=x^2+y^2$; $Circ.=2\pi R$. These are formulas of quantitative identity, of equality. They are not attained by generalization of matter, but in entire abstraction of matter; they have no material content. They are not generic of things, and do not serve as premises in material reasonings. They furnish abstract forms in which concrete matter may be cast. To apply mathematical forms to matter is the special function of Applied Mathematics. To make an application of a formula is not to draw an inference from it, but merely to supply it with a content of suitable matter. Material inferences are not made from, but according to, a formula.

Precisely the same is true of logic. The Aristotelic *Dicta* express merely syllogistic form (§ *93*). Every material syllogism concludes, in Fig. 1, not from, but in accord with, these canons. They are often spoken of as the ultimate major premises in material reasonings. This is an error. They serve only to express the abstract form in which sound reasoning concerning things proceeds.

What in this respect is true of deduction is true also of induction. In its formal character induction evolves abstract canons and formulas, deduced from axiomatic principles, which canons and formulas in ordinary affairs and in the inductive sciences are supplied with concrete, material facts and things.[1] In all cases the inductive inference is made, not from a form, but according to or in conformity with a form. The notion that the axiom of uniformity is the ultimate premise in induction is false and confusing. A material conclusion comes always and only from one or more material premises, in conformity with certain established abstract forms.

§ 32. We maintain, then, that the inductive process consists wholly and exclusively in a direct immediate inference authorized by the principle of uniformity, an inference so simple that in making it a formal fallacy is well-nigh impossible. This inference is not reducible to syllogistic form. The attempt results either in a violation of syllogistic law, and thus is false reasoning, or it presents forced

---

[1] The canons of causation, to be hereafter discussed (§ 55 sq.), are likewise deduced from the axioms previously laid down, and are merely abstract formulas of causal relations.

It is remarkable that there should be need to explain the relation of form to matter, when these words are in familiar and accurate use in every-day life, even children and the vulgar using them in correct distinction. E. g. The form of the oration was good, the matter poor. But logicians, whose specialty it is to mark and regulate the distinction, often either ignore or reject it; hence the need of exposition and insistence.—Cf. § 2 and § *4*, and *Theory of Thought*, p. 5.

forms, quite unnatural and therefore untrue. For, we repeat, it is the general function of logic to evolve the forms according to which actual thinking is naturally and rightly accomplished; and its special function is to state and demonstrate these forms clearly and distinctly, so as to dissipate the obscurity in which they usually lie, even in minds otherwise highly instructed.

Why, it may fairly be asked, if the process of induction is so simple and infallible, should there be an elaborate treatise on the subject. Were the formal procedure alone to be considered, we might stop at this point, having discussed the definition of induction, its principles, and the character of the process. Still the ground and manner of its material applications would need discussion, especially when taking the form of laws, more especially laws of nature.

But there is much else to be expounded. The preparation and complete establishment of the premise from which to infer inductively is a process of the highest importance, and often of very great difficulty. This process also must therefore be sharply defined, hedged in by rules or methods, and provided with canons and formulas; thereby constituting a large and the most intricate part of inductive logic. This preparation for the induction, so far as it involves inference, is itself strictly deductive, and results in establishing a causal relation between particular phenomena. When accomplished, then the inductive generalization, a single simple step, takes place. Its result, a universal truth, perhaps a law, affords a settled major premise from which deductions may be made by subsuming special or particular cases, thus enlarging science in its details.

For instance, Newton made long and laborious deductions from observations, and thereby settled the particular fact that the earth and moon attract each other directly as the mass of each and inversely as the distance squared. This preparation accomplished, he then, according to logical order, inferred inductively the universal law of gravitation. Subsequently modern astronomy has been developed chiefly by deductions from this law. Thus the intermediate inductive step, while all-important, is single, very simple logically, being immediate, and is justified by the principle of uniformity.

IV.—OBSERVATION

§ 33. The ground of induction, furnishing matter to be formalized, is experience (§ 6).[1] The object known in experience is a phenomenon. A phenomenon is whatever appears, presented either to the external or to the internal senses. It is the undetermined object of empirical intuition. There are two great classes of phenomena, those of coexistence and those of succession.

Phenomena of coexistence are exemplified in the figure of a body, and in the comparative figures of separate bodies. Such relations are conditioned on space and the geometrical properties of space alone; for, being characterized by simultaneity, they are independent of time. Thus, that a sphere is two-thirds of a cylinder whose height is equal to the diameter of each, is uniformly true in all cases without regard to time. Very many phenomena of coexistence are referable to causative antecedents; as, high tide on opposite sides of the earth. Other coexisting phenomena are not so referable, but are ultimate; as, the ultimate properties of substances. Water has

---

[1] "So that the art and practic part of life
Must be the mistress to his theoric."
—*K. Hen. V.*, act i., sc. 1.

many such properties which always coexist, so that when we recognize it by some of them, we are sure of the presence of all.

Ultimate uniformities of coexistence, not being referable directly or remotely to causation, are not subject to the principles and methods of induction. They are, however, subject to observation and classification, thus forming the basis of kinds, especially of natural kinds, and thus coming, not under causal law, but under definition. Hence the various kinds of rocks and minerals, and of chemical compounds, expressed by a general name and its definition; as, *Marble is crystalline carbonate of lime;* also the natural kinds of plants and animals. These have ultimate coexisting properties which science obtains by analysis, and recognizes as constituting the original nature of the things, and furnishing the basis of generalization and classification (§ 5).

Phenomena of succession are conditioned on time, and are subject to the laws of causation and induction. Such phenomena are by far the more numerous and important. On a knowledge of them and their laws is founded every scientific explanation of past events, also every reasonable anticipation of future events, and whatever power we possess of influencing these to our advantage. They constitute the chief subject of our subsequent inquiries.

§ 34. Attention to a phenomenon and to its attendant phenomena or circumstances is observation. This implies more or less mental analysis of a whole into its constituent parts, and their classification. When we open our eyes on a landscape, there is an experience of vision; what is seen is a whole, whose parts are quickly distinguished and classified as mountains, streams, forests, buildings, and so on. These are kinds of things. They are observed as coexisting phenomena. A storm arises, clouds gather, rain pours, lightning flashes, thunder rolls, the bolt has riven an oak or fired a dwelling, a whirlwind threatens yet greater ruin. These are classified as kinds of events. They are observed as successive phenomena, and are recognized as causally related. Thus observation is discriminating attention.

Observation has two modes distinguished as simple observation and experiment. The former takes place when a phenomenon happens to fall under notice, or when, without acting upon it, we seek and find one suited to our ends. The latter takes place when by an artificial arrangement we produce a suitable instance, and by this action bring it under our observation. The distinction is clear, but does not imply a logical difference. The character and value of a fact is not at all affected by the way it is ascertained. The practical difference, however, is important, and requires consideration.[1]

---

[1] The verb *to experiment* always implies activity, while *to experience* suggests rather a passive, receptive state, and thus is more nearly allied to simple observation. Both words are from the same deponent verb *experiri*, to try or to be tried. We try an experiment (Ger. *Versuch*), we undergo an experience (*Erfahrung*). But experience and

§ 35. A phenomenon being given, its cause or its effect is to be ascertained, as a preliminary to induction. In other words, before a scientific induction can be made, a problem is to be solved: either given an effect to find its cause, or given a cause to find its effect. Observation, therefore, must extend beyond the given phenomenon to its circumstances, eliminating those that are immaterial (§ 16), and distributing the remainder as antecedents and consequents. To do this thoroughly and accurately is often difficult, requiring great care and skill.[1]

When an effect is given to find its cause, only simple observation is applicable. Seeing that a bit of silver chloride has turned from white to black, and inquiring the cause of this change, we are limited to simple observation of the circumstances. We can-

observation are here used synonymously, and as generic of simple observation and experiment. All imply voluntary attention, which is essentially active. While perception, taken strictly, is passive, there is no passive observation.—See *Psychology*, § 82 sq., and § 99.

[1] The elimination of immaterial circumstances will be considered subsequently (§ 51). No useful rule can be given for the distribution of the antecedents and consequents. In general, what has been, changes, and ceases to be, we should reckon an antecedent; what was not, eventuates, and begins to be, we place among the consequents. "It happens sometimes that when a relation of causation is established between two facts, it is hard to decide which, in the given case, is the cause and which the effect, because they act and react upon each other, each phenomenon being in turn cause and effect. Thus, habits of industry may produce wealth, while the acquisition of wealth may promote industry. As Plato remarks, education improves nature, and nature facilitates education. National character, again, is both effect and cause; it reacts on the circumstances from which it arises."— Lewis, *Methods of Politics*, i., p. 375.

not take an effect and try what will cause it, we cannot reverse the order of nature. We can only make note of the circumstantial and substantial antecedents, knowing that the cause is in them. We may further observe the phenomenon amid various circumstances, and so be able to eliminate many that are not causal conditions, and thus reach a conclusion more or less probable. In this way we might find that the like change in several specimens of silver chloride is probably due to light.

If it happen that two cases occur wherein all antecedent circumstances are strictly alike except that in one case an antecedent is present with the phenomenon in question and in the other both are absent, then we have scientific proof that this antecedent is the cause of the phenomenon. If two quite similar bits of silver chloride are observed under quite similar circumstances except that one is exposed to light and the other not, then the fact that only the former has turned black is proof that light is the cause. It is rare, however, that simple observation is so happy as to find two such cases, or even a series of cases varying sufficiently to satisfy the demands of scientific proof, nature being constituted on quite a different plan from that of facilitating our inquiries.

When a cause is given to find its effect, experimental observation is often applicable; but there are many cases, indeed whole sciences, whose matter is of such sort as to be mostly, if not wholly, out of the reach of experiment. The mental sciences admit it but sparsely, though recently some progress has been made in experimental psychology. Anthropology, zoology, geology, and astronomy are sciences whose ground is almost exclusively simple observation. Thus it is that, in looking from effect to cause, we are in all cases limited to simple observation by the nature of the relation; and in looking from cause to effect, we are in many cases limited to simple observation by the nature of the matter.

§ 36. Experimental observation, though applicable only to the problem of given a cause to find its effect, and in this natural order only to matter that can be handled, is nevertheless an extension of observation, since it multiplies the facts. Also it is a means of more exact scientific knowledge. Indeed, simple observation, which when alone hardly yields sure knowledge of causal relations, has its best results in furnishing ground for supposition, and in suggesting intelligent experiment. When in its exercise we have found reason to suppose that the blackening of silver chloride is the effect of light, we have recourse to experiment, reversing the order, and testing the influence of light upon the salt. We hereby extend observation, and determine with precision the cause of the phenomenon.

In the previous section it is indicated that the observation of a phenomenon in various circumstances leads approximately to the determination of its cause or of its effect, by means of the successive elimination of circumstances that are immaterial. Now, it is a prerogative of experiment to vary the circumstances at will, and thus intelligently to produce precisely the sort of variation that conduces most definitely to the determination we seek, a variation which perhaps nature does not furnish at all. In order to know which of the two principal components of air, oxygen and nitrogen, supports combustion and respiration, we separate them, thus bringing them into states not found in nature; then testing one and then the other with burning and breathing things, we ascertain, by this especial variation of circumstances, that oxygen is the effective component.[1]

Moreover, when we can produce a phenomenon artificially, it may be isolated, or at least produced amid circumstances which are well known, and hence not liable to be confused with it. For the study of magnetism, a house is built apart, with no

---

[1] One hundred years before Bacon's time, Leonardo da Vinci, the painter and scientist, wrote: "Theory is the general, Experiments are the soldiers.... We must consult Experience, and *vary the circumstances* till we have drawn from them general rules; for it is she who furnishes true rules. But of what use, you ask, are these rules? I reply that they direct us in the researches of Nature and the operations of Art: they prevent our imposing upon ourselves and others. ... Nature begins from the Reason and ends in Experience; but, for all that, we must take the opposite course: begin from the Experiment and try to discover the Reason."—Venturi, *Essai*. Bacon emphasized "the prerogative of experiment," and urged compliance with Nature: "*Natura non aliter quam parendo vincitur.*" Coleridge is more inquisitorial. To experiment is "to bind down material matter under the inquisition of reason, and force from her, as by torture, unequivocal answers to prepared and preconceived questions."—*Friend.*

iron in its construction, so as to avoid local disturbance. Instead of simply observing electricity in thunder-clouds, we evolve it in a room by means of contrivances that are sufficiently understood, such as the Holtz machine, a voltaic battery, or a dynamo. A hospital is the best place for studying disease, for the surroundings and treatment of patients are largely under control of the physician. When the phenomenon in question is thus insulated, we proceed to test it by introducing some well-defined circumstance, and noting the consequents. A chemist, having obtained apart a new element or compound, applies various well-known reagents in succession, and observes what unions or disunions take place. Such practical isolation of a phenomenon, and the testing it with various familiar and modifying circumstances, thus determining definitely its causal relations, is perhaps the most important prerogative of experimental observation.

V.—ENUMERATION

§ 37. The first form of induction to be considered is one that is in very common use and highly important; natural and right under certain provisos and limitations, but to be distinguished from scientifically prepared procedure. It is described by Bacon as *Inductio per enumerationem simplicem, ubi non reperitur instantia contradictoria*. This, he says, is the only mode of induction that was known to the ancients, or indeed prior to his time.

It is of two kinds. One arises from a simple enumeration of cases that resemble each other in a given mark or marks; the other, from a simple enumeration of marks in which given cases resemble each other. The one is an inference from a count of similar instances or cases; the other is an inference from a count of similar qualities or marks. The one deals with matter relatively to its extension; the other relatively to its intension (§ *20*). The former is called enumeration of cases; the latter, analogy.[1] Of these in their order.

---

[1] Analogy is not recognized by Bacon as a kind of simple enumeration. It is usually treated by subsequent logicians as a distinct mode of inference, sometimes as hardly inductive. The logical place and relation here assigned will be justified by its treatment in the sequel (§ 41 sq.).

§ 38. The frequent recurrence of an observed fact gives rise in the mind to expectation of its renewal. This by the laws of suggestion.[1] Indeed, a single fact strongly impressed does likewise; as, *A burnt child dreads fire.* The irrational brute mind seems to act in this respect like the human mind. But the human mind reaches a higher plane when, having observed certain repetitions, it concludes inductively a general truth. That *All crows are black* will be stoutly maintained by a boor, and not without reason, he never having seen a contrary case. We have no other proof that *All men are mortal,* and the admitted certainty that you and I shall die is a deduction from this inductive generalization based on enumeration.

The formal procedure of induction by an enumeration of cases may be expressed in the following CANON: **If many instances agree in having two marks in common, then all instances having one have also the other mark.**

The process is formulated and exemplified thus: If $A, B, C, D, E \ldots$ are observed to have each the marks m and n, we make the induction that all cases having m have also n. Then X, being seen to have m, is deductively inferred to have an unseen n. Newton observed that many highly refractive (m) substances, as oils and resins, are combustible (n). Through inferring it of all, he reached the further conclusion that the diamond, being highly refractive,

---

[1] For Laws of Suggestion, see *Psychology,* § 172 sq.

is also combustible, which was afterwards verified (see § 47). The inductive step takes this form:

> Some specific cases agree in an accidental mark;
> ∴ All such cases agree in this accidental mark.

In making the induction the mark generalized is regarded as a logical accident; as, *All metals are lustrous* (§ 5). But further investigation may conclude it to be essential; as, *Cows ruminate, All animals have a nervous system;* in which case the mark is transferred to the definition of the kind.

§ 39. What justifies this form of induction? There is in the human mind a natural and strong tendency to generalize from observed repetitions, but the only principle that will justify a generalization beyond experience is the principle of uniformity. This is the basis of every induction. All men know that like causes have like effects, with the inverse, and though very few may have thought it in abstract form, still when a uniformity is observed, when two or more facts frequently and invariably concur, these are at once suspected to be causally related, either as one determining the other, or as coexisting parts of a consequent. Which or what is the cause may be quite unknown and unquestioned, but an obscure surmise, more or less reliable, that the concurrence is due to causation, is the authority for the induction.

If I see a number of men in succession rush by my window up the street, instinctively I wonder what is the matter. I cannot, perhaps, even guess. Nevertheless, I expect the next one that passes will follow the others; having deduced his case from the induction that, for some cause or other, everybody is running up the street. On cold, clear nights in the north the aurora has frequently appeared, hence at such times Northerners watch for it. So we all expect meteors in November, and confidently predict the zodiacal light in February. Should a comet appear with a coma not turned from the sun, astronomers would be more bewildered than ever. In case of a hemorrhage of the lungs, the doctor promptly administers a dose of common salt. Why? All that he knows, or that any one knows, is that this old woman's remedy has often been efficacious. The inference to *all*, which is the inductive step, is sometimes so obscurely and quickly passed through that it escapes the attention even of logical analysts, and the whole process seems to be a direct inference from particular to particular; as when a village matron says: "This physic cured my Susan, therefore it will cure your Lucy." But there is surely an intermediate universal.[1]

General rules, sometimes called laws, obtained by induction from a mere enumeration of cases, are known as empirical rules or laws; for, the causes being unknown, at least in their *modus operandi*, the induction is made solely on the experience of the cases, without investigating the surmised causes,

---

[1] For the contrary view, see Mill, *Logic*, p. 141 sq.

and so no explanation by reference to more general laws is assignable. The practice of medicine is very largely thus empirical (§ 95).

§ 40. What is the value of such imperfect induction?[1] In the practical affairs of every-day life its value is inestimable. General truth that has been or can be scientifically determined is insufficient for the needs of the scientist, and is unknown to the vulgar; hence in the vast majority of even most important concerns we are obliged to use induction from enumeration of cases as the only available means to guide expectation and provisory conduct. The hazard that attends it is often great; still, by an extensive multiplication of facts, no exception occurring, we are able to infer reliable rules. Not one person in thousands has any other reason for believing that the sun will rise to-morrow, that the moon will change, that the seasons will come and go in fixed order, that industry secures reward, that no one is content, that money purchases goods, that physic cures, that water quenches thirst, or even that he himself can walk and talk.

While this form of induction can never furnish scientific proof of a universal proposition, but at best only yields high probability, yet, even in its less

---

[1] The custom is to call the Aristotelic procedure discussed in § 27 perfect induction, though truly it is not induction at all, and all induction proper imperfect induction. I prefer to call induction by enumeration imperfect induction, and induction by methods yet to be expounded perfect induction.

conclusive instances, it has great scientific value in serving constantly to suggest causal relations, thus pointing the way to investigation by the sure methods which are to be hereafter discussed. Thus the diurnal ebb and flow of the tide, observed for ages, led at last to the investigation that proved the moon to be the cause.[1]

§ 41. To induction by a simple enumeration of cases corresponds induction by a simple enumeration of marks, or analogy.

[1] It is quite evident that the mode of induction before us rarely gives rise to satisfactory knowledge. "Popular notions," says Mr. Mill, "are usually founded on induction by simple enumeration; in science it carries us but a little way. We are forced to begin with it; we must often rely upon it provisionally, in the absence of means of more searching investigation; but for the accurate study of nature, we require a surer and a more potent instrument."—*Logic*, p. 227. It is surprising, after so excellent a statement, to find this highest authority holding and laboring to prove that the "ground of induction" is grounded on enumeration. See *supra*, § 19, note. In this palpable diallelon (§ *146*) he is followed, as in other respects, by Mr. Bain.—*Logic*, bk. iii., ch. xi., § 13. Mr. Venn admits the logical fault, but comes to the rescue with a psychological justification.—*Logic of Chance*, ch. x., § 14.

Bacon strongly condemns induction by simple enumeration as unscientific, as "*mera palpatio*." He says: "Inductio quæ procedit per enumerationem simplicem res puerilis est, et precario concludit, et periculo exponitur ab instantiâ contradictoriâ, et plerumque secundum pauciora quam par est, et ex his tantummodo quæ præsto sunt, pronunciat. At Inductio quæ ad inventionem et demonstrationem Scientiarum et Artium erit utilis Naturam separare debet, per rejectiones et exclusiones debitas; ac deinde, post negativas tot quot sufficiunt, super affirmativas concludere."—*Nov. Org.*, bk. I., aph. 105. Cf. aph. 25 and aph. 69. Mr. Mill quotes approvingly the same passage "as a final condemnation of this rude and slovenly mode of generalization."—*Logic*, p. 549.

Analogy is liable to be confused with metaphor. The latter, taken in a wide sense, is a rhetorical form wherein, because of some resemblance between two things, the marks of one are transferred to the other. Because they are alike in courage, we say: *Achilles is a lion.* So also: *There is a tide in the affairs of men, etc.; Age is the evening of life; Gratitude is the memory of the heart; A ship ploughs the sea; James, Cephas, and John were pillars of the church.* Such similitudes are used to adorn and to illustrate, but are inconsequent, and give rise to a fallacy (§ *140*). Analogy likewise is founded on resemblance, and the name is often very loosely applied to any and all similes. But as a logical form, analogy is restricted to such resemblances as are consequent, furnishing ground for logical proof.[1]

According to its early definition, analogy is an equality of relations. For example: *As is a father to his children, so is a ruler to his subjects.* Here we have stated, in an equality or identity of relations, the paternal theory of government, from which may be deduced the duties of citizens.[2] But it is now usual and better to extend the logical

---

[1] Metaphor (from μετα-φέρειν, to transfer) is a mental transference of marks. Analogy is not a transference of marks, but because some marks are observed to be inherent, other marks are inferred to be inherent, which is not transference, but inference.

[2] With Aristotle analogy is ἰσότης λόγων, an equality of relations. His example is: ὡς γὰρ ἐν σώματι ὄψις, ἐν ψυχῇ νοῦς.—*Eth. Nic.*, I., vi., 12. Formally this is a proportion, an equality of ratios. In mathematics the term analogy is still used in this restricted sense.

meaning of analogy to any resemblance, not merely of relations, but of things and classes of things, that justifies an inference of further resemblance.

§ 42. Accordingly we have already defined induction by analogy as an inference from a simple enumeration of marks in which given cases resemble each other (§ 37). A sportsman has found trout in a deep pool of a clear brook. On coming to another pool, very similar in many observed respects, he makes the induction by analogy that it is similar in yet other respects; thence he deduces the probable presence of trout; and casting in his line, proceeds to verify the case. Solid metal is marked by a peculiar lustre; hydrogen has many metallic qualities; hence, through an induction by analogy, it is highly probable that, should hydrogen be solidified, it would exhibit metallic lustre.

The formal procedure of induction by an enumeration of marks may be expressed in the following CANON: **If two instances agree in having many marks in common, then all marks in the one are also in the other instance.**

The process is formulated and exemplified thus: If A and A' are observed to have many marks in common, we pass by analogy beyond this experience, and infer all their marks to be common; then, having noted that A has a mark m not seen in A', we deduce its presence there. The evidence that brutes are consciously intelligent is analogical. There being very many physical points notably common to man and brute, the induction is to all points, making allowance for differences of degree; and thence is deduced, what cannot be directly observed, the conscious intelligence of the brute. It is usual to say that brutes show signs of conscious intelligence by certain actions; but these actions are merely transient marks obviously common, which are accepted as analogical signs in the brute of a deeper mark beyond observation. Let it be noted that the complete analogical argument here illustrated consists of two steps, an induction followed by a deduction. The first step being obscure, is usually overlooked, and hence the inference seems to pass immediately from particular to particular.

When the two cases under consideration are of the same kind, an essential mark belonging to the definition of the kind evidently cannot be made the occasion of analogical inference. Only marks considered accidental are inferable by analogy. The inductive step takes this form:

Some accidental marks agree in two specific cases;
∴ All accidental marks agree in these two cases.

This may yield a fuller knowledge of the essence. Some, many, accidental marks are common to oaks and pines. Then, from an induction of all, we conclude that, since oaks are observed to be dicotyledonous, pines are so likewise. This, verified by observation, has been adopted as a generic mark.

Generally the same result may be obtained by either mode of enumeration. The conclusion that

I am mortal may be had thus: My neighbor and I being much alike, and he dying, then I too shall die. So also Newton's inference that the diamond is combustible (§ 38) may be represented analogically. This might be expected from the striking similarity of these two forms of induction, and from the convertibility of extension and intension to which they severally correspond (§ 37).

§ 43. The justification of an inference by analogy, like that from an enumeration of cases, lies in the principle of uniformity. The sole support of the induction is the knowledge or surmise, however obscure, that the marks observed to coexist in the one case are causally connected, and hence may be inferred to coexist in the analogous case. Hence, if the observed property or mark m be known to be unconnected causally with any of the properties of A in which A' resembles A, there is no basis for analogical inference. On the other hand, if the mark m be known to be connected causally with some one of these properties of A, the imperfect induction by analogy is superseded by a perfect induction (§ 40 n.). We must be measurably assured that m is connected causally with some of the resembling properties without knowing with which it is so connected.

It is evident that if the induction from *some* correspondences in the two cases to *all* were fully authorized, the result would be one of entire identity; also that cases are hardly ever so thoroughly assimilated. The *all* of the induction, therefore, can be taken only in a loose and doubtful sense even when no contraries are observed, and the deduction from it is at best doubtful. If, along with an observed community of many marks, there is also an observed disparity of others, these as against those proportionally diminish the probability of the inference. When the differences balance the resemblances, analogy affords no presumption.

There are striking points of community between the senses of smell and taste, and also of hearing and seeing, which have led by analogy to a fuller knowledge of them.[1] Sodium and potassium have many points of agreement and few of difference; there is, therefore, considerable probability that a newly observed quality of one has its counterpart in the other; or, since qualities are causes, that an effect due to sodium might also arise from potassium, such as the rapid decomposition of water at ordinary temperature. An instance may thus have the mark of being a cause or an effect.

Plato's Republic, whose constitution is modelled by that of the individual man, is a brilliant ideal; but to infer from three leading functions of mind that there should be three classes of citizens in the state is inept, for these are not counterparts. Yet, when we observe that pure reason is legislative, thought judicial, and will executive, and thus discover in human nature the approved functions of departments of state, the resemblances are sufficient

---

[1] These analogies are more fully stated in "*Psychology*, §§ 9, 20.

to justify an inference by analogy to others that are derivative.

A famous analogical argument is, that, since the earth and the moon have many points of resemblance, and the earth is peopled, therefore the moon also is peopled. To this it is properly objected, first, that being peopled cannot be surmised as the effect even remotely of any or all the enumerated resemblances; secondly, that the points of difference are much more numerous and weighty than the resemblances, and therefore the presumption is decidedly to the contrary. If we substitute Mars for the moon, the resemblances are increased and the differences diminished, but still the argument fails. A better analogical inference is that the stars, like the sun, are attended by planets.[1]

§ 44. Analogy renders good service in practical concerns by furnishing useful hints that sometimes ripen into maxims or rules of life. It helps to a good guess, is an index to truth. The balsam of Peru, besides many other properties, is medicinal; the balsam of Tolu agrees in many of those properties, and presumably may replace the other in pharmacy. But such inferences standing alone are very hazardous. The order of plants *Solanaceæ* is defined by many common points. It includes the tomato, potato, and egg-plant, which are wholesome food. To

---

[1] See the anonymous essay, usually attributed to Dr. Whewell, entitled "Of the Plurality of Worlds."

infer this of all other species would be perilous, for the order includes the thorn-apple, tobacco, and also belladonna or deadly-nightshade, a virulent poison.

To establish any scientific doctrine whatever analogy of itself is quite insufficient. The brilliant treatise entitled "Natural Law in the Spiritual World,"[1] whose argument in support of its leading doctrine, indicated in the title, is only and can only be from analogies, has not widened the domain of science or increased its treasures. Still, the process has scientific value. It may often profitably be used to confirm a truth otherwise ascertained, and thus become ancillary to science. It is useful too in tentative or provisional classifications, as those of the Linnæan botanical system. But its principal service is to suggest lines of research by certain conclusive methods to be considered hereafter. The points of community between hearing and seeing suggested to Huyghens and to Young, that, as hearing is the effect of external vibrations of an elastic medium, so seeing might perhaps have a similar cause. Thus by analogy originated the hypothesis of an undulating luminiferous ether.

Analogy has also a negative but great scientific value in meeting objections, and thus is a useful defensive instrument. The argument of the masterly treatise entitled "The Analogy of Religion to the Constitution and Course of Nature"[2] shows that the difficulties in religion, natural and revealed, have the

---

[1] By Henry Drummond, F.R.G S.   [2] By Bishop Joseph Butler.

same relation to their respective systems that the difficulties in the course of nature have to the entire system of nature. If, then, the latter be admitted to proceed from a divine Author, the difficulties in the former are not a valid objection to a like origin. In this statement the analogy is represented expressly as an equality of relations (§ 41). It may be stated also thus: Nature and religion are largely analogous—that is, have many likenesses, even as to difficulties; if, notwithstanding these, a divine Author is attributed to the former, He cannot, because of them, be consistently denied to the latter. It is not intended to prove the divine origin of religion, but indirectly to confirm proper proofs by showing that the difficulties in religion, being like those admitted by the deist to exist in nature, cannot be offered by him as an objection to its divine origin. The procedure is evidently *ad hominem* (§ *108*).

VI.—PROBABILITY

§ 45. It has several times been stated that enumeration furnishes only probable evidence. Let us now examine the meaning of probability, and consider its bearing.

To probability is opposed certainty. Only intuition and demonstration, as in pure mathematics, are attended by pure or strict certainty. Demonstration starts with and results in certainty, for its ultimate premises are intuitive necessary principles, and it carries their strict certainty into its conclusions. The process is always a deduction, for it proceeds from the strictly universal to the less general. Both deductive and inductive logic, like pure mathematics, deduce their formal theorems or canons from intuitive necessary principles; the process is demonstrative, the results strictly certain, admitting no degrees.[1]

But the application of the theorems of logic to empirical matter involves, as in applied mathematics, the essential uncertainties of experience (§ 8), as well as those arising from the imperfect fulfilment of the theoretic conditions. It is clear that any uncertainty in the premises is followed by an equal uncertainty

---

[1] On the feeling of certainty, see *Psychology*, §§ 69, 118, 227.

in the conclusion (§ *91*). Hence in the employment of induction especially, since the material application of its formal theorems depends wholly on experience, strict demonstrative certainty is unattainable.

Probable evidence is distinguished from demonstrative by admitting degrees from the lowest presumption upward, but not reaching strict certainty. That the tide ebbs and flows to-day affords a slight presumption that it will do so to-morrow; and the evidence gathers force with each added observation, until the observations of ages, no exception occurring, afford by enumeration alone inductive proof of high order, giving strong assurance that it will do so again, but not giving certainty in its strict sense. Events falling within this wide range are regarded as merely more or less probable.

Having set probability apart from strict certainty, let us narrow its range by a further distinction. Besides strict or pure certainty we recognize physical and moral certainty, the former relating to natural, the latter to human, events.[1] These together may be called empirical certainty. When an order of facts has been proved by a rigorous application of the determinative methods yet to be discussed, it is scientifically ascertained, and is said to be physically or morally certain as the case may be—that is, empirically certain, and not merely probable. Here, then, is the

---

[1] Moral certainty, an objectionable phrase, usually quite indefinite, but too well established to be changed or rejected. The meaning to which we here limit it is justified by the etymology of moral, from Lat. *mos, moris,* manner, custom, habit, conduct.

upper limit of probability. Its extent is from the lowest presumption having any, the slightest, evidence in its favor, up to the physical or moral certainty, the empirical certainty, of scientific truth. That the sun will rise to-morrow is not strictly certain, but is physically certain. That, when the sunset sky is red, the morrow will be clear, is not a scientifically ascertained sequence, but has at best only some degree of probability.

§ 46. Comparatively few phenomena in nature, still fewer in human affairs, present themselves in a form suited to close scientific investigation. By far the greater number, often those of the highest practical moment, are out of reach of scientific treatment, and our knowledge of them and our conclusions from them are uncertain. These fall within the wide range lying between bare conjecture and empirical certainty, the range of probability. In such matters we are dependent on imperfect unscientific induction, merely approximate generalization, such as is yielded by enumeration. This probable evidence, in its very nature, affords but an imperfect kind of information, yet on a vast multitude of occasions we have no other resource in guiding our conduct. The ability to judge fairly of probabilities distinguishes the man of wide experience, close observation, and practical sagacity. When pronouncing what is likely to be true—that is, like in evidence or circumstances to some known truth or true event—he rarely errs.

"It is observation that produces, in numberless

daily instances, a presumption, opinion, or full conviction that such an event has or will come to pass; according as the observation is that the like event has sometimes, most commonly, or always, so far as our observation reaches, come to pass at like distances of time or place, or upon like occasions. Hence arises the belief that a child, if it live twenty years, will grow up to the stature and strength of a man; that food will contribute to the preservation of its life, and the want of it for such a number of days be its sure destruction. So likewise the rule and measure of our hopes and fears concerning the success of our pursuits, our expectations that others will act so and so in such circumstances, and our judgment that such and such actions proceed from such principles—all these rely upon our having observed the like to what we hope, fear, expect, judge. And thus it is that to us probability is the very guide of life."[1]

"Even when science has really determined the universal laws of any phenomenon, not only are these laws generally too much encumbered with conditions to be adapted to every-day use, but the cases which present themselves in life are too complicated, and our decisions require to be taken too rapidly, to admit of waiting till the existence of a phenomenon can be proved by what have been scientifically ascertained to be the universal marks of it. To be indecisive and reluctant to act, because we have not evi-

---

[1] Butler, *Analogy*, Int.

dence of a perfectly conclusive character to act on, is a defect. If we would succeed in action, we must judge by indications which, though they do not generally mislead us, yet sometimes do, and we must make up, as far as possible, for the incomplete conclusiveness of any one indication, by obtaining others to corroborate it. The principles of induction applicable to approximate generalization are therefore not a less important subject of inquiry than the rules for the investigation of universal truths." [1]

§ 47. The hazardous validity of the canons of enumeration is conditioned on there being no known exceptions, *instantia contradictoria* (§ 37). In an application to a material case, though no exception may have been observed, and though we may feel assured from the extent of the observations that if there were an exception we should have met with it, still, since we can never be positive of this, it follows that a universal by enumeration is never more than probable. We surmise, and perhaps strongly suspect, the observed uniformity to be due to causation wherein a real exception is impossible; as, *Horses eat grass, Cows chew the cud, Birds lay eggs;* [2] but when quite ignorant of the determining causes, though feeling

---

[1] Mill, *Logic*, p. 417.

[2] Such invariable attributes sometimes come to be regarded as essential marks of natural kinds, and then are posited as generic defining qualities; as, *graminivorous, ruminant, oviparous*. In such case to say, for example, that *All birds lay eggs* is merely to refer to the definition, and is not an induction.

sure of their existence, we can do no more than venture a highly probable universal proposition.

The saying that a real exception to a causal uniformity is impossible is simply a varied statement of the irrefragable principle of uniformity, and when a real exception occurs we know at once that the phenomena in question are not causally related. Before giving up our probable universal, however, we should be very sure the exception is real, and not merely apparent (§ 8). Merely apparent exceptions frequently occur, due to the presence of some counteracting circumstance, some modifying or preventive cause; as, when gunpowder fails to explode, being damp (§ 15). Exceptions of this sort do not invalidate the induction, its universality being always under the general condition: *Provided there be no preventing cause.* We do not lose faith in a medicinal specific because it sometimes fails to cure. But any exception rightly checks expectation. We hesitate, and recognize the hazard of procedure.

But when a real exception has been detected, this observation of a contrary forbids the induction of a universal proposition. The best we can say is *Some* (a few, or many, or most, but not all) *A's are B;* as, *A few springs are silicious; Many strata are fossiliferous; Most clays are ferruginous.* Such incomplete uniformities of coexistence are not, cannot be, cases of causation, and hardly rise to the dignity of empirical maxims, much less of laws. The predicate is contingent, the coincidence fortuitous. An approximate generalization of this sort positing *Most are*, or

Most are not, obviously requires a comparative knowledge of the total, the observed cases being a majority. The assertion when limited to these observed cases is not an induction, but merely a partial colligation (§ 9), and affords no ground for even a probable inference to unobserved cases. We may only say that perhaps, perchance, possibly, others correspond. Newton inferred from oils, resins, etc., the invariable concurrence of high refrangibility with combustibility, and thence deductively predicted the combustibility of the diamond (§ 38). This haply proved true. But, as Brewster remarks, had he known the high refractive power of the minerals greenockite and octohedrite, and made the prediction of them, it would have failed, they being real exceptions invalidating the induction, and showing the concurrence to be by chance. Facts that thus concur by chance do not come within the range of probability indicated in § 45, but lie below in a logical region which we shall now examine, preparatory to a rise from it through probability into empirical certainty.

§ 48. It has already been said that a chance or fortuitous event, a pure accident, a hap, a casualty, in the sense of an uncaused event, is impossible in fact, or even in thought (§ 18). There is no such thing as chance, in antithesis to cause or law, in the whole realm of being. So taken, the word has no meaning whatever.

Every event is the effect of causes, and might be predicted from a knowledge of them. The turning up of a particular card is a causal consequence of the way the pack is handled, and of the place of that card in the pack; this last is a consequence of the way the cards were shuffled; and so on. When a leaf, loosened from its stem, falls to the ground, its final position is strictly determined by causes operating chiefly during its descent through the resisting air. Every natural event is physically necessary, but not physically certain, for there are many that, in our ignorance, we can neither predict nor explain.[1] Such wholly uncertain events are called casual, or are said to occur by chance. The word chance is thus used as a common name for the unknown cause of any single occurrence; as, *The tree fell by chance due north*. To say, then, that any one phenomenon is produced by chance is merely a conventional mode of expressing our ignorance of its cause, and in this sense the word has no place in logic.[2]

---

[1] The statement that each natural event is physically necessary means that it is causally determined to be just what it is, without possible alternative. This is quite apart from our knowledge and belief respecting it. Physical certainty, as described in § 45, has reference to knowledge and belief. Certainty and uncertainty are primarily states of mind, and are attributed secondarily as marks to a recognized relation among objective facts, when the relation so far as known is such as to produce some degree of one or the other mental state in the observer. It is evident that a complete knowledge of the real relation involving physical necessity would be attended by strict certainty, and that any inferior degree of certainty is due to a corresponding measure of ignorance. See the references in § 45, note; and Whately, *Logic*, Appendix I., iv.; also Thomson, *Outline, etc.*, § 122.

[2] Says Aristotle: δοκεῖ μὲν αἰτία ἡ τύχῃ, ἄδηλον δὲ ἀνθρωπίνῃ διανοίᾳ.—*Physica*, ii., 4.

But when two or more phenomena or events, that are in no way related through causation, coexist or succeed one another, they are said to concur by chance. In this sense we shall find use for the word. Examples of such concurrence are: *We met by chance;* and, *The night of Cromwell's death, a violent storm broke over London.* Also, *We chanced to arrive an hour apart;* and, *The appearance of the great comet of* 1861 *was followed by war.* Some such casual coincidences may recur again and again; as, *Many great battles have happened on Sunday.* Chance in this sense may be defined as the possibility of an event, and the problem of chance is to estimate the value of this possibility in terms expressing the likelihood of its recurrence.

§ 49. The logical doctrine of chance, then, proposes to estimate the relative value of a chance. The clearest illustrations, perhaps, are drawn from games of chance. In these the probabilities are artificially balanced; in other words, there is no probability either way. Take a toss of a penny. Head or tail? It must be one or the other, but it is impossible to predict which, since there is no ground for probability in favor of the occurrence of either.[1] Still,

---

[1] The terms chance and probability are very often used synonymously; as, by Laplace in his "Essai Philosophique sur les Probabilités," and by Mr. Venn in his "Logic of Chance, an Essay on the Theory of Probability." In the present treatise we prefer to distinguish them. Probable cases are those that have some evidence, more or less, in their favor. The probabilities may be either for or against an

we are sure that, in the long run of many throws, the number of heads and tails will be about equal. No specific experience seems prerequisite to this assurance.

How are we assured, without trial, that the chance between the two is even? According to the axiomatic principle of Sufficient Reason, nothing comes to pass without a reason why it should occur in that way, rather than in another.[1] But, in the case supposed, we are acquainted with the causes at work sufficiently to know that there is nothing, no constant cause, giving a bias in the long run to either face of the penny; that is, there is no cause furnishing a sufficient reason for inequality. Therefore, inequality will not come to pass; or, in the long-run, equality of heads and tails is reasonably expected.

event—that is, an event is probable or improbable according to the evidence of causal connection or repugnance. Chance is not a species, but a pure negation of probability, occupying the indifferent mean between the probable and improbable. It is strict uncertainty.

[1] Leibnitz, who introduced this principle into logic, says in a letter to Dr. Clarke: "In order to proceed from mathematics to natural philosophy, another principle is requisite (as I have observed in my 'Theodicæa'). I mean the principle of the *sufficient reason ;* or, in other words, that nothing happens without a *reason* why it should be so, rather than otherwise. And, accordingly, Archimedes was obliged, in his book 'De Equilibrio,' to take for granted that if there be a balance, in which everything is alike on both sides, and if equal weights are hung on the two ends of that balance, the whole will be at rest. It is because no *reason* can be given why one side should weigh down rather than the other." The reference is to *Theod.*, i., § 44. See Mr. Venn's modified view, *Logic of Chance*, ch. iv., § 8 sq. Evidently the principle of Sufficient Reason is merely an imperfect statement of the Laws of Causation, § 18 sq.

Upon this *a priori* reasoning, whose subsumption, however, is empirical, is based the doctrine of the calculation of chance. "The calculation in general consists in reducing all events of the same kind to a certain number of cases equally possible, that is, such that we are equally undecided as to their existence; and in determining the number of these cases which are favorable to the event of which the chance is sought. The ratio of that number to the number of all the possible cases is the measure of the chance; which is thus a fraction, having for its numerator the number of cases favorable to the event, and for its denominator the number of all the cases which are possible." [1] We will consider two species.

First.—*When the uncertain events are taken severally, the chance of recurrence is expressed by the number of cases favorable to it, divided by the whole number of possible cases.* In tossing a penny 2000 times, we reasonably expect each face to recur about 1000 times. In every single toss, each of the two possible cases is equally possible—that is, equally uncertain. The chance, then, of either face recurring is $\frac{1}{2}$. So likewise in case of drawing a ball from a bag containing an equal number of black and white balls, or, in general, in casting equal lots in any manner.[2] A die,

---

[1] Laplace, *Essai sur les Probabilités*, p. 7.

[2] The remarkable parity of male and female births, statistically ascertained, fixes the chance of each at $\frac{1}{2}$. The parity of male and female deaths is an obvious deduction from the parity of births. The

having six faces, the chance of an ace, or any other number, is $\frac{1}{6}$; which is only a mode of saying that in many throws, for instance 600, the ace would recur about 100 times. Also in each throw the chance against an ace is $\frac{5}{6}$. If there be in a lottery wheel five prizes in every hundred lots, then the chance of drawing a prize is .05, or $\frac{1}{20}$; and the chance of drawing a blank is .95, or $\frac{19}{20}$.

Second. — *When the uncertain events are taken together, the chance of their concurrence recurring is the product of the separate chances.* When a pair of dice is thrown, the chance of an ace with each die being $\frac{1}{6}$, the chance of double aces is $\frac{1}{6} \times \frac{1}{6} = \frac{1}{36}$, which is also the chance of an ace twice in succession with a single die. The chance of cutting a coat-card of the twelve in the pack of fifty-two is $\frac{12}{52}$ or $\frac{3}{13}$; hence, of doing so twice in succession, $\frac{3}{13} \times \frac{3}{13} = \frac{9}{169}$. Let the first of three urns contain two black and four white balls, and the others six white balls each. What is the chance of drawing a black ball? The chance of the drawer taking the first urn is $\frac{1}{3}$. In it the black balls are $\frac{2}{6}$ of its whole number of balls. Hence the chance of a black ball is $\frac{1}{3} \times \frac{2}{6} = \frac{1}{9}$. Syllogistically: *A is $\frac{1}{3}$ C; B is $\frac{2}{6}$ A;* ∴ *B is $\frac{1}{9}$ C.* Note that if the eighteen balls were in one urn, the chance would be the same.

Mathematicians have greatly extended these principles, and added others, making application to a

---

census bulletin of April 27, 1894, shows that in the U. S. males constitute about 51 per cent. of the population.

great variety of cases, and have thus elaborated a logico-mathematical system known as the Theory of Chance.[1] Its practical applications, however, are not considerable, nor does its study seem to cultivate sagacity in the estimate of that probability which is "the very guide of life."[2] We have touched upon only the simplest elements, and these merely with a view to their immediate bearing on the general theory of probability.

§ 50. To set apart casual from causal coincidence, we need a canon for guidance, since the distinction is important and often difficult to mark. Absolute frequency of concurrence will not suffice. Some events that invariably concur are merely casual; as, every change of fortune in one's life concurs with some change in the position of the planets, but we no longer believe in planetary influence. On the other hand, some events that only occasionally concur may be causally connected, the failures being due to unobserved counteracting circumstances; as, rain only sometimes concurs with an east wind.

---

[1] The "Essai" of Laplace, quoted above, and that of Quetelet, "Sur les Probabilités," are the standard authorities.

Besides works already referred to, the "Formal Logic" of Professor De Morgan should be named; also Quetelet's "Essai de Physique Sociale," and his "Anthropométrie."

[2] "Never did I know," says Bulwer, "a man who was an habitual gambler otherwise than notably inaccurate in his calculations of probabilities in the ordinary affairs of life. Is it that such a man has become so chronic a drunkard of hope that he sees double every chance in his favor?"—*What Will He Do with It?* ch. x.

From a fact as indefinite as this last example nothing can be inferred. Let us suppose, however, that rain concurs about as often with east wind as with any other; then it is presumably a chance concurrence. But if rain concurs more frequently with east wind than with any other, this indicates that one can under certain circumstances cause the other, or something cause both. If the concurrence is less frequent, this indicates that one, or some cause of one, can counteract the other. The form of this procedure, distinguishing casual from causal phenomena, is expressed in the following

Canon: **Estimate the positive frequency of each of the phenomena, and how great frequency of coincidence would take place, if there were neither connection nor repugnance. Then, if the facts correspond, the coincidence is presumably casual. If there be greater frequency, there is presumably causal connection; if less, causal repugnance.**

To estimate the positive frequency of a phenomenon we strike an average on an extended series of observations. This fixes the ratio between its occurrence and its failure to appear. Also it eliminates mistakes of the senses, accidents, and all errors that do not arise from some permanent bias. Suppose we thus ascertain that the phenomenon a occurs once for two instances of the general circumstances, and that b occurs once for three. These are their positive frequency.

Now, if a and b be independent, the average frequency of their coincidence will be once in two times three, or six, instances; and hence, if the observed coincidences be to the instances as one to six, the coincidence is presumably by chance (§ 49).

But if the observed coincidence is more frequent than one time in six, there is presumably some cause tending to produce it; if less, some cause tending to prevent it. The probability of concurrence will increase or diminish with this greater or less frequency.

If, in a certain locality, during the spring months, it shall have been observed for a number of years that rain (a) occurs as often as every other day, also that an east wind (b) occurs as often as every third day, and that they concur on the average once in six days, then there is presumably no causal relation between them—it is a chance concurrence. But if the observed concurrence be more frequent or less frequent, it is evidence of causal relation.

To vary the illustration: If, in another locality, fair weather should occur twenty times as many days in the year as not, and westerly winds three times as often as not, then, were there no connection or repugnance, fair weather in the long run would concur with westerly wind five times in seven; for $\frac{20}{21} \times \frac{3}{4} = \frac{5}{7}$. Now, if the actual concurrence be six in seven, it is probable that one tends to produce the other, or that there is some common producing cause; if four in seven, that one tends to prevent the other, or that there is some occasional preventing cause.

The principle applies to an enumeration of marks

or analogy. When the coincident marks in two cases are greater or less in number than chance would afford, we infer that they are causally related, and make a probable induction respecting unobserved marks. The East Indian and the English languages have more common points of syntactical construction, and similar names for the same things, than chance will account for, which analogy indicates a common origin. This renders it probable that other similar features are discoverable, so that the existence of some peculiarity in the one justifies a search for its analogue in the other. The differences between English and Arabic are greater than chance would yield; hence a probable repugnancy in fundamental construction, and an expectant search for still other divergences.

§ 51. The principle involved in the foregoing canon furnishes ground for the elimination of chance.

In the first place it distinguishes a series of concurring phenomena having real exceptions from such as have only apparent exceptions (§ 47). As the former does not justify induction, it is, when exposed, set aside as the result of chance—eliminated as unfitted for inductive investigation. That many great battles have happened on the Sabbath day is an historical fact from which nothing can be inferred; for a count would doubtless find them to be one-seventh of all—a mere chance, yet striking coincidence.

In the next place the canon helps us in complex cases to distinguish and eliminate the chance accompaniments of a phenomenon undergoing investigation. Every phenomenon occurs to observation amid circumstances that are immaterial—that is, having no causative relation to the case. Many of these are eliminated by the plainest common-sense; as, in a chemical experiment in the wet way, it is immaterial whether the containing vessel be glass or porcelain. Many are eliminated by isolating the phenomenon as far as possible, and producing it experimentally amid well-known circumstances (§ 36). Still some usually persist whose presence, though invariable, has no bearing on the case, and whose absence would not modify it. The relative position of the planets was believed by the alchemists to exert an important influence on experimental combinations. The chemist of to-day is sometimes embarrassed by persistent accompaniments which are really chance concurrences, and so need not be regarded. Observation of the phenomenon in various situations, artificially varying the circumstances when practicable, is a means by which, according to the canon before us, immaterial, chance circumstances may be detected, and then eliminated from consideration. This process is especially important as preliminary to a search for the cause or effect of a phenomenon by the scientific methods to be considered subsequently.

An obvious example of the elimination of casual circumstances is the common-sense explanation of the progress of the seasons. The fluctuations of temperature from day to day due to meteorological change are chance accompaniments, which, being eliminated, leave the corresponding progress of the sun from solstice to solstice as the one determining or causal antecedent. The sure profits of a faro-bank, having a capital too large to be broken by a run of bad luck, are explained in like manner; for, eliminating the chance elements, there remains, in the very constitution of the game, a small but permanent advantage in favor of the banker, which in the long-run insures his winnings. In all so-called games of chance which nevertheless involve skill, as whist, success in the long-run falls to the skilful players.[1]

An elimination of the chance elements of a complex phenomenon occasionally discovers small and hence unsuspected though permanent causes. A series of throws will detect a loaded die by the turning up of a certain face oftener than chance will account for. The slightly more than chance errors of an instrument of precision indicate some minute permanent bias, for which, when determined, allowance must be made. In this way the obscure diurnal variation of the barometer was discovered. An elimination of its grosser meteorological fluctuations from many daily observations, brought it to light and measurement.[2]

---

[1] Judge Gaynor, now of the Supreme Court of New York, decided (1894) that horse-racing is not a lottery within the legal definition any more than in common speech. The opinion says: "A lottery depends on a lot or a chance, such as the casting of lots, the throwing of dice, or the turning of a wheel. In a race the horse-owners pay a sum, not to win a larger sum by lot or chance, but in order to enter into the contest of skill, endurance, and speed upon which the stake depends."

[2] Even with the best instruments of precision, strict accuracy can-

§ 52. The preceding considerations prepare us to examine more definitely the valuation of probabilities. It has already been stated that when a uniformity is noted by the enumeration of only a few instances, there is a slight presumption in favor of an inductive universal; and that as observations varying in circumstances multiply, no contrary case occurring, the probability increases until it reaches the highest degree, bordering on physical or moral certainty (§ 45). A deduction from a universal by enumeration, subsuming some particular unobserved instance, is attended by all the hazard involved in the universal; and if the particular differs considerably from the observed instances in its circumstances, the deduction, even from a highly probable

---

not be expected in a single observation. Therefore it is usual to make a large number of observations, and, by an application of the Method of Least Squares, to approximate very closely and surely the true value. For the best instruments of precision are subject to variations. Heat, with its irregular warping influence, draughts of air, dust and consequent friction, distortion by strains, and the slow uneven contraction of metal which continues long after casting—all these cause deviations. Moreover, every instrument is liable to some permanent bias, due to imperfect construction, which vitiates results, and therefore must be ascertained and eliminated from each observation.

Another form of permanent bias lies in the observer, some mental disposition inclining him constantly to perceive in a case more or perhaps less than is real. Add to this the special action of his muscles and nerve currents. Allowance must be made, especially in minute observations on quantity, for the personal bias of each observer. Its value is expressed in what is called his "personal equation," which phrase has become familiar to us in connection with astronomical observations. It is ascertained only by comparing the results obtained by various observers of the same or similar phenomena.

universal, becomes so precarious as to have little value.

It has also been stated that the discovery of a real exception invalidates the universal (§ 47). The Zulu of a century ago believed no doubt that *All men are black*. To *All swans are white* there are unaccountable exceptions. The satellites of Uranus and Neptune retrograde, and so invalidate *All members of the solar system move eastward*. Such are cases of overhasty generalization, a fault of every day and every hour, acknowledged by the Psalmist in "I said in my haste, *All men are liars*."

Exceptions not known to be real, and hence presumably only apparent, do not invalidate the universal, since it is conditioned on the proviso that no interference or prevention takes place. A modifying or disturbing cause or force may be always present, and in some cases prevail, becoming a preventive cause. That all terrestrial bodies fall to the ground from a given height with like velocity is not invalidated by the retarding effect of the ever-present air, nor falsified in the case of an ascending balloon. The expression is rendered unexceptionable and still more general by saying that all bodies *tend* so to fall. Thus a tendency, even if never realized, may be recognized as universal. The generalities of Mechanics are rendered more exact by expressing them in terms of tendency to motion, or pressure.[1]

---

[1] "The habit of neglecting this necessary element in the precise expression of the laws of nature has given birth to the popular prejudice

But instances more or less liable to frustration by unrecognized interferences yield only a questionable universal, under which the subsumption of an unobserved particular differing much in its circumstances is precarious, and the conclusion only more or less probable. The Greek church has flourished chiefly among the Slavonic races, the Roman among the Latin, the Protestant among the Teutonic. Hence an affinity may be presumed between these several forms and the character of the races. Change of time, place, or circumstances, as lapse of centuries, emigration, political revolution, often breaks this uniformity. It is at best an empirical generalization, whose application to unobserved cases yields only a low degree of probability.

Approximate generalizations that are not mere colligations of observed cases (§ 47), but are inductions proper, extending beyond experience, are usually expressed by *Most are* or *Most are not*, or their equivalents; as, *Most Judges are incorruptible*. Otherwise we say that the proposition is true in general, or generally, which in usage implies that exceptions are recognized at least as possible; as, It seems to be generally true that *Every man has his price*, that *The wealthy are more virtuous than*

---

that all general truths have exceptions; and much unmerited distrust has thence accrued to the conclusions of science, when they have been submitted to the judgment of minds insufficiently disciplined and cultivated. The rough generalizations suggested by common observation usually have exceptions; but principles of science, or, in other words, laws of causation, have not."—Mill, *Logic*, p. 319.

the indigent, that *Punishment deters from crime.* A statement of provisos, when complete, converts the very general into a universal proposition; as, *An absolute sovereign will abuse his power,* unless his position depend on the good-will of his subjects, or unless he have great rectitude and resolution, or unless he be guided by a minister having these qualities. So also, *Honesty is the best policy,* provided it squares with current opinions, promotes public interest, and is displayed to view. The value of the probability involved in such generalities cannot be exactly, numerically estimated. It taxes the sagacity of the experienced observer to judge their worth in general statement, and in application to special or particular cases. They abound in practical affairs, and are largely the guide of public and private conduct.[1]

It should be noted that induction by enumeration very often arises from groups of instances, extends to similar groups, and thus becomes more reliable, attaining a higher degree of probability. Thus, if in many observed groups containing A's, most A's are B, then in all groups containing A's, most A's are B. If in various counties of Virginia most farms grow

---

[1] The form of the argument is: *If x is, y is; but y is;* ∴ x (probably, presumably) *is.* This is recognized as a fallacy when the relation is that of reason and consequent (§§ *91, 119, 145*); but when, as here, the condition is causal (§ *110*), it affords a probability, a presumption in favor of the conclusion. For the allowed plurality of causes (§ 22), which investigation reduces, alone forbids the *sine qua non* reading: *Only if x is, y is,* which would yield ∴ x *is.* See § 59.

tobacco, then in all counties most farms grow it; or, simply, most farms in Virginia grow tobacco. The inference from observed groups to similar unobserved groups is more probable than inference to individuals.

§ 53. An indefinite judgment of probability is frequently expressed definitely, borrowing the language of chance, in the form of a ratio; as, *It is ten to one that a drunkard cannot be reformed;* and, *Not more than one person in a hundred forms independent opinions in politics or religion.*[1] Such statements are inaccurate, but, making an approach toward a measure of probability, are significant of degree. The statement that *As likely as not he will consent* is an inference from some one's character to his conduct as wholly uncertain. A turf-gambler will bet two or more to one on his favorite racer, according to his judgment of the ratio of probabilities.

An accurate numerical expression of probability, like that of chance, is practicable in many instances both of natural phenomena and of human affairs,

---

[1] "What Hobbes says of Charles II.—

'Nam tunc adolescens
Credidit ille, quibus credidit ante Pater'—

is true of the vast majority of men even in the most enlightened countries. Hence a strong probability that any given individual has never exercised any independent judgment in politics or in religion. A hundred to one is a safe estimate of such a probability."—Bain, *Logic*, bk. iii., ch. xiv.

with the modification that the positive frequency of the phenomenon can very rarely if ever be known *a priori* (§ 49), but must be ascertained by observations reduced to actual count. For example, all the metals are white, including shades of gray, except two, copper and gold. As chance will not account for this, we presume there is some modifying cause in the atomic constitution of these exceptions which determines the difference. Now, since there are fifty known metals, the probability that hydrogen, when liquefied, will be white is as 50 to 2. In general, then, if we know the exact proportion of instances in an approximate generalization, we can state numerically the degree of probability of an inference from it. If there be no exceptions to a well-ascertained uniformity, the probability is at its maximum.

An actual count, extensive and exhaustive, thus enables us to express probabilities with scientific precision. Herein lies the inestimable value of statistics. Statistical estimates and investigations, with a view to setting up an inductive universal, or at least a general rule, successfully strive by what is improperly called a wide induction of facts, properly a wide enumeration of cases, to approximate the certainties of exact science. Our decennial census makes a wide count of very many matters relative to the lives, property, resources, and occupations of the people. These are reduced by the Census Bureau, averages struck, and ratios obtained, which, through induction, justify inferences of great value, especially to the immediate future.

For illustration, let us suppose that in a given county the average number of annual deaths in ten years is found to be two per cent. of the population; then we may confidently infer that in the next decade a like per centum of mortality will prevail, provided the population, mode of living, etc., are not materially changed. This inference is from one temporal group to another. It would be equally competent to infer the same per centum of mortality of an adjoining analogous county for either decade. We remark that the inference is indifferent as to order of time, since it would be true likewise of the previous decade, but that it is greatly weakened if applied to a case differing considerably in time, place, or circumstances. Also we remark that, while this inference from group to group, temporal or spatial, may reach the highest probability, it furnishes no ground for inference respecting the life of any individual member of a group.

Such statistics as to term of life, loss by fire, shipwreck, and the like, furnish a safe basis on which to calculate the value of risks, and so justify the investment of large capital in the business of insurance. For example, the American Tables of Mortality show the results of wide and accurate statistical observation. Among other averages they give the expectancy—that is, the probability—of life for different ages. A healthful man at 20 years of age has an expectancy of 42 years more; at 30, of 35 years; at 40, of 28; at 50, of 21; at 60, of 14; at 70, of 8. The rates charged by a life-insurance office for a policy of $1000 increase as the expectancy decreases. It is quite obvious, yet needing to be stated, that the probabilities of life thus estimated are of no assurance to the individual person insured, but only to the office insuring. The inference from the large group statistically estimated as to mortality to the large group the office has in hand holds good, those who die short of expectancy being balanced on the average by those who live beyond it, and by this means the office knows in advance with high probability the amount from year to year of its disbursements, and rates its charges to correspond.

VII.—DIFFERENCE

§ 54. In view of the foregoing discussion of induction by enumeration it is plain that, were there no surer canons, the prospect of attaining scientific truth of unquestionable universality would be hopeless. The radical defect of enumeration is that in this preparation for induction there is only a surmise that a determining cause exists, not an ascertained knowledge of the actual determining cause. Consequently, by conforming to its stated canons, we reach only a tentative, somewhat probable, but still, except in the rarer cases, hazardous, generality. Induction grounded on enumeration is truly induction, but imperfect, always falling short of empirical certainty (§ 45).

A knowledge of the cause or effect of a phenomenon is scientific knowledge, as stated in the ancient aphorism: *Scientiă est rerum cognoscere causas.* Such knowledge is a sure foundation for induction, and prerequisite to perfect induction characterized by empirical certainty. In undertaking now an examination of the several methods by which this preliminary knowledge is sought, it will be well at the outset, for the sake of clearness, to express formally the governing principle of the induction which it conditions. This principle is derived directly from the primary Laws of Causation, being, indeed, merely a slight modification of the Axioms of Uniformity (§§ 19, 21). It may properly be termed the General Canon of Perfect Induction, reading thus: CANON: **A cause and its effect being known, from all like causes like effects are inferable, and from all like effects like causes are inferable.**

Hence it is evident that, in logical order, before the induction takes place, a preparatory problem is to be solved: either, a particular cause being given, to find its effect; or, a particular effect being given, to find its cause. When this is done, the induction, expressed in a strictly universal proposition, is, according to the canon, immediately inferred.

§ 55. The several methods of solving the preparatory problem constitute one of the chief considerations of inductive logic, and their application is the chief difficulty in scientific investigation, the subsequent inductive step itself being an immediate inference of the simplest character (§ 26). They are quite commonly called "inductive methods," though not themselves inductive, but merely preparations for induction, methods for ascertaining causal relations between phenomena. To their exposition we are now about to proceed. It will be found to consist in the proof, statement, and illustrative application of several Canons of Causation, or canons of methods for the determination of causal relations, canons which express merely the forms of thought to which actual processes must conform. These, like the canon of induction just stated, are evolved *a priori*, are derived deductively from the Laws of Causation. They should not be mistaken for canons of induction, since they are strictly and solely the formal processes by which a particular fact of causation may be ascertained, formulating only a sound and scientific preparation for subsequent inductive procedure.

The methods are primarily two—the Method of Difference, and the Method of Agreement—each having subordinates. Both accomplish their ends by a partial elimination of circumstances, in order to detect which particular circumstances are concerned in the causation. In the Method of Difference, whatever circumstance cannot be absent without the absence also of the phenomenon under investigation, is causally connected with that phenomenon; in the Method of Agreement, whatever circumstance can be absent without the absence also of the phenomenon under investigation, is not causally connected with that phenomenon. These maxims are obviously derived from the Axiom of Change (§ 18), which furnishes the basis of the methods.[1]

---

[1] The methods of scientific investigation now before us are all essentially methods of elimination, and thus conform to Bacon's aphorism that induction proceeds "by due rejections and conclusions."—*Nov. Org.*, i., 105, already quoted in § 40, note. This process Bacon contrasts with the method of "simple enumeration," and justly claims to be the first to make it prominent; but his "Prerogatives of Instances," id., bk. ii., hardly anticipate the present methods.

§ 56. The most important, direct, and simple method for determining the causal relation between phenomena is the Method of Difference. It is

Newton's four "Rules for Philosophizing" (§ 21, note) are quite different from these methods, and have special reference to his own procedure in the "Principia."

Sir John Herschel, in his "Discourse on the Study of Natural Philosophy," gives, in § 145, five "general rules for guiding and facilitating our search, among a great mass of assembled facts, for their common cause." From the rules he deduces nine "propositions readily applicable to particular cases." Four of these (2, 7, 8, 9) are the four methods, though lacking the prominence given them by Mr. Mill as the sole and sufficient methods of logical proof. By Herschel the four propositions indicated, together with the others, are expounded as aids to discovery; the notion that they constitute a system of logical proof does not seem to have occurred to him. Of his admirable "Discourse" Mr. Mill says: "It is a work replete with happily selected exemplifications of inductive processes from almost every department of physical science, and in which alone, of all books which I have met with, the four methods of induction are distinctly recognized, though not so clearly characterized and defined, nor their correlation so fully shown, as has appeared to me desirable."—*Logic*, p. 297.

Science in all its branches is deeply indebted to Mr. Mill for the first clear and distinct statement of its logical methods, and the importance now universally attributed to them is mainly due to his influence. It was the distinction of his "System of Logic" to draw a clear and broad line between the Art of Discovery and the Science of Proof. The latter is Logic. It is concerned mainly with methods of proving propositions, and only in an incidental way does it aid in suggesting them. He says: "The business of Inductive Logic is to provide rules and models (such as the syllogism and its rules are for ratiocination) to which, if the inductive arguments conform, those arguments are conclusive, and not otherwise. This is what the four methods profess to be, and what I believe they are universally considered to be by experimental philosophers, who had practised all of them long before any one sought to reduce the practice to theory."—*Logic*, p. 308.

The Canons of Causation, as we have designated them, of the pres-

based, as just stated, on the Axiom of Change, from which are deduced the following special maxims:

1st. When a consequent appears or disappears, and with it an antecedent, the latter is the cause or a part of the cause of the former.

2d. When an antecedent cannot be introduced or excluded without adding or losing a consequent, the latter is the effect of the former.

These deductions are comprised in the following CANON OF DIFFERENCE: **If an instance wherein a phenomenon occurs, and another wherein it does not occur, have every circumstance in common save one in the former, this is wholly or partly the cause of the phenomenon, or its effect.**[1]

A symbolical formula of this canon is as follows:

$$A\ B\ C \qquad\qquad B\ C$$
$$y\ z\ x \qquad\qquad x\ y$$

The larger letters represent particular causal antecedents, or simply causes; the smaller letters, particular consequents or effects. Each of the larger letters usually stands for a collocation of distinguishable but co-operating factors; each of the smaller,

---

ent treatise, are the "Four Methods of Experimental Inquiry" drawn from Mill, "Logic," bk. iii., ch. viii. In transcribing them, we have ventured to rearrange them and to make some verbal changes in the interest of logical order, brevity, and precision.

[1] It should be noted that in this, and in the subsequent Canons, an *instance* or case is an observed total analyzed into antecedents and consequents (§ 35); some one or a group of these is the *phenomenon* under investigation, and the rest are its *circumstances*.

for a collective fact. The two groups represent two instances or cases, one instance affirmative and one negative of $A\ z$. If z be the particular phenomenon under investigation, the fact that it disappears in the second instance along with A proves that A, either alone or together with some other antecedent, is its cause. If A be the phenomenon under investigation, the fact that it cannot be absent, as in the second instance, without the loss of z, proves that z is its effect.

Such is a formal statement in theoretical strictness of the method of difference, a process of elimination. It should be observed that, although in its practical applications only approximate results can be obtained, yet it is the most rigorous proof of particular causes or effects that is possible, and when its theoretic conditions are fairly fulfilled its results are empirically certain, falling little short of strict demonstration, and thereby furnish a safe premise for induction (§ 26).

§ 57. Material examples in general accord with this formal method lie on every hand. It is unwittingly used daily and hourly even by the most thoughtless and ignorant persons. We cite several common-sense cases.

I see rain (z) falling, and a cloud (A) in the sky; the rain disappears, and with it the cloud; I infer this cloud to be the cause, at least in part, of that rain.[1]

[1] It may be well to recall just here our doctrine on the function and

A sound (z) strikes my ear (x), and I see a swinging (A) bell (B); the sound ceases, and with it the swinging; I infer that the swinging was partly the cause of the sound. There is here no induction; but I might inductively infer, *All swinging bells always produce sound.*

If I find my dog shot through the heart, I know, by the method of difference, it was this that killed him; for he was alive just now, and all circumstances are the same except the wound. Again no induction; one might follow, but would be superfluous.

A scientific and more recondite example is as follows: When looking in a spectroscope at the spectrum of incandescent sodium (A) and calcium chlorides, I see a very bright yellow line (z); just now, when looking at the spectrum of incandescent calcium chloride, this yellow line was absent; I infer that in the present case the incandescent sodium is the cause of the bright yellow line. Then may follow an induction of all such cases.

The foregoing are inferences from effect to cause. An inference in the reverse order is: I observe a shower of hail (A), and, on going to my conservatory,

---

application of form, § 31. The canons now before us are merely formal statements, without any material content. They do not serve as premises from which material conclusions are inferred, but in their application the provided abstract form is merely supplied or filled in with given matter. Thus the forms *instance, phenomenon, circumstance*, are simply embodied, in the above example, by *weather, rain, cloud.*

find the glass broken (*z*); I infer, all other circumstances being unchanged, that the breakage is the effect of the hail. Also, just before the hail, I observed a cold nor'wester set in, and infer that the hail was its effect.

So a pilot, noting that during a thunder-storm the needle was disturbed, and that during a storm without lightning it was not disturbed, concludes the disturbance to have been effected by the lightning.[1]

§ 58. The illustrations thus far given are cases of simple observation, and to this we are limited when an effect is given to find its cause (§ 35); but when a cause is given to find its effect, we may have recourse also to experimental observation. Simple observation of nature often fails to discover, amid her vast complications, the second case requisite to fulfil exactly the conditions of proof by this method, but when we have an approximation indicating the causal relation, or a suggestion of it from some other quarter, we may, if the matter be subject to handling, apply the test of experiment (§ 36).

The conclusion of the pilot, stated above, may be

---

[1] The method of difference is applicable also to inquiry concerning preventive cause (§§ 15, 47). A patient has intermittent fever (*z*). If in the interval he be brought under the influence of quinine (*A*), the fever does not reappear, the quinine acting as a preventive cause, though we are puzzled to know how. Here *B C* is followed by *y z x*, and *A B C* by *y x;* that is, in the presence of *A*, *z* disappears; hence *A* counteracts *B C* so far as to prevent the effect *z*. So, also, as the old wives tell us, a silver spoon (*A*) in a common tumbler will prevent its breaking (*z*) when it is filled with hot water. This, too, puzzles us.

tested, inverting the order of proof, and verified thus: Place a copper wire near and parallel to a magnetic needle, the latter is not disturbed; electrify the wire, instantly the needle is disturbed, taking position at right-angles to the wire; therefore this disturbance is effected by the electricity. Note that this test verifies, not the particular conclusion of the pilot, but an obscure induction from it, that *Electricity deflects the needle.*

The previous spectroscopic instance may be tested and verified, reversing its order of thought, by this experiment: Produce the spectrum by an incandescent platinum wire, the bright line does not appear; having touched a pellet of sodium with the point of the wire, produce the spectrum, instantly the bright yellow line flashes across; therefore it is the effect of the incandescent sodium.

Again, wishing to ascertain which of the two chief components of air supports breathing life, we put a mouse in an open jar, and then fill the jar by displacement with pure nitrogen; the mouse soon dies; therefore nitrogen is azotic, and it is the oxygen of the air that supports life.

Thus the method of difference is pre-eminently a method of experiment, and the most potent means of scientific investigation. To it the student of nature always preferably resorts in cases where its application is possible. Perhaps nine-tenths of the experimental research in the chemical, physical, physiological, and other scientific laboratories, as well as the testing of ordinary matters, is by the method of difference.

Let it be remarked that the foregoing examples of the method are not inductions. So far as they involve inference, it is deductive. The result in each case is merely that a certain particular fact is the cause, or the effect, of a certain other particular fact. The method of difference only prepares this ground for the induction of a universal according to the general canon of induction (§ 54). An inductive inference is then competent, and is so simple and direct that thought almost instinctively makes it, indeed running constantly before the proof of the particular with an anticipating generalization. It requires, therefore, some attentive discrimination, rarely exercised on this point even by logicians, to avoid confusing the preparatory process with the logically subsequent induction.

§ 59. Recurring to the first example in § 57, we inductively infer, *Every like cloud always causes rain.* Here *rain*, a generalized effect, is attributed to *cloud* as its generalized cause. The statement is in the form of a causal, categorical, universal proposition. Letting *A* stand for any generalized cause, and *z* for its generalized effect, we have:—

If *A* is, then *z* is; and
If *z* is, then *A* is.—Canon, § 54.

These may be combined in the compound form:—

Only if *A* is, then *z* is.

This implies, not merely that if either is, the other is, but also that if either is not, the other is not.

Hence affirming either affirms the other, and denying either denies the other. Such is the character of the causal conditional, *causa essendi*, as distinguished from the logical conditional, *causa cognoscendi* (§ *110*). Formally and theoretically it is rigidly *conditio sine qua non*.

Now suppose that, having obtained inductively a universal, some new particular phenomenon of like sort is observed, then it may be subsumed, and an unobserved fact deduced, as follows :—

    Only if A is, then z is;
    But A is; | But z is;
    ∴ z is | ∴ A is.—Ponens.

E. g. When I see just such a cloud in the distance, I conclude it is raining over there; or, when at night I hear the rain on my roof, I conclude there is a rain-cloud above. Again :—

    Only if A is, then z is;
    But A is not; | But z is not;
    ∴ z is not. | ∴ A is not.—Tollens.

E. g. If there be no such cloud, there is no rain; or if there be no rain, there is no such cloud. Other forms of the so-called conditional syllogism may be used in these deductions (§ *119 sq.*).

§ 60. A modification of the foregoing method of difference is the Method of Residue. After the principal causes of a complex phenomenon have been severally ascertained, there often remains a portion unaccounted for. Sometimes this is so slight as to be overlooked, or else supposed to be due to errors of observation. But alert scientists have learned to scrutinize with profit what others neglect. Indeed, some very important discoveries have resulted from the study of an apparently trifling residue. Separating it from the cognate effects, inquiry is made for a corresponding surplus in the antecedents, which has either been disregarded, or is as yet unknown, and this, when found, is rightly posited as the cause of the residuum. The formal process in such case is expressed succinctly in the following CANON OF RESIDUE: **Subduct from a complex instance the consequents of ascertained antecedents, and the residue is the effect of the remaining antecedents.**

The method may be formulated as follows:

$A\ B\ C$	But B	and C	$\therefore B\ C$
$y\ z\ x$	x	y	$x\ y$

Here the complex instance has yielded to investigation that x is caused by B, and y by C. On subducting x and y from the total consequents, a residual phenomenon, z, perhaps quite inconspicuous, is discovered. This, then, is the effect of A, the remaining antecedents.

Note that the two instances, one affirmative and one negative of $A\ z$, characteristic of the method of difference, appear in the formula. This negative instance, however, is not obtained by direct observation, but is deduced from the effects which B and C produce separately. Still the method is as cogent as the method of difference itself, provided the premises $B\ x$ and $C\ y$ of its specific deduction are obtained by that method, and that A is the only agent to which z can be referred. Otherwise further proof is requisite.

§ 61. For example: Arfwedson, in 1818, on analyzing a portion of a certain mineral ($A\ B\ C$), whose total weight ($y\ z\ x$) he ascertained, found the weight (x) of the contained magnesia (B), and the weight (y) of other components (C). Subducting these weights (x and y) from the total, a residue (z) was observed. Searching the mineral for its cause, he discovered a substance (A), previously unknown, and named it lithia. In like manner were discovered iodine, bromine, selenium, and several new metals accompanying platinum.

The discrepancy between the observed and calculated times of eclipses of Jupiter's satellites was a residue accounted for by the difference of times requisite for the passage of light, previously supposed to be instantaneous, over his greater and less distances from us, and on this basis Roemer calculated its velocity.

The perturbation of the planets was a residue which led astronomers to extend the law of gravitation from the central body, to which alone it was at first supposed to be applicable, inductively to all bodies in the universe.

The geologists who posit early cataclysmic causes allege in support of their view that, after the effect of all ordinary causes has been allowed for, there is a large residue of facts proving the existence in geologic eras either of other forces, or of like forces greatly intensified.

Whoever claims that there is a fundamental difference in the intellectual capacities of the sexes should show that, after subtracting from the known differences all that can be attributed to differences of physical organization and to the influence of environment, there is a residue which can be attributed only to an ulterior distinction.

VIII.—AGREEMENT

§ 62. It has already been said that the ordinary course of nature or of affairs rarely presents cases fulfilling the requirements of the method of difference. Moreover, it often happens that these requirements cannot be fulfilled by experimental contrivance with sufficiently rigorous accuracy. In such cases an alternative mode of discovering the cause of a given effect, or the effect of a given cause, is afforded by the Method of Agreement. This method follows the maxim that whatever circumstance can be absent from a case without the absence also of the phenomenon under investigation, is not causally connected with that phenomenon (§ 55). It is based on the Axiom of Change, from which are deduced the following special maxims:

1st. When a consequent disappears without the disappearance of a given antecedent, the latter is not the sole cause of the former.

2d. When an antecedent disappears without the disappearance of a given consequent, the latter is not the effect of the former.

3d. The antecedent and consequent, which together are constant during the successive disappearance of each of the others, are related as cause and effect.

These deductions are comprised in the following CANON OF AGREEMENT: **If instances wherein a phenomenon occurs have only one circumstance in common, this is its cause, or its effect.**

A symbolical formula of this canon is as follows:

$$A\ B\ C \qquad A\ B\ D \qquad A\ C\ E$$
$$y\ z\ x \qquad s\ y\ z \qquad x\ z\ v$$

If z be the particular phenomenon under investigation, the fact that the three instances containing it have only one circumstance in common, the antecedent A, is evidence that A is the cause of z. Conversely, if A be under investigation, the common consequent z is its effect.

In the application of this method the instances are studiously varied so as to eliminate in turn the several chance or immaterial circumstances attending the phenomenon (§ 51). We must follow the Baconian rule of "varying the circumstances"; for a repetition of strictly similar cases, however numerous, proves nothing, there being no elimination. Only dissimilar cases eliminate, and so afford proof; hence these should be multiplied as far as needful.[1]

---

[1] The enormous extent to which experiments are sometimes carried in order to establish causal connection finds illustration in physiological investigation by vivisection. M. Paul Bert describes a series of experiments extending to No. 286. Flourens states that Magendie used 4000 dogs in an effort to prove Sir Charles Bell's theory of the motor and sensor functions of the nerves, and, having failed, used 4000 more to disprove it; but that he himself had proved Bell to be right by the vivisection of 1000 more.

The questionable possibilities will thus be gradually reduced in number, and, if the means of elimination be complete, the inquiry terminates in fixing upon some one circumstance that has never been absent when the phenomenon is present.

§ 63. Newton observed bright prismatic colors (z) displayed in white light on a film (A) of a liquid soap-bubble; like colors in white light on a film of solid mica; like colors in white light on a film of air between glass plates. The only common circumstance appearing to be white light on a film, he posited this as the cause of the prismatic colors, now more fully explained by the interference of light.

Conversely, cause being given to find its effect, if in several instances an alkali and oil (A) unite, e. g. potash and tallow, soda and suet, lime and olive oil, a common circumstance is soap (z); this, then, is the effect of the common antecedent.

From each of these particular determinations an induction is now competent, thus: *Any transparent film in white light exhibits prismatic colors;* and *Any alkali and oil uniting produce a soap.*

Some other examples will be helpful. We observe in many cases the conversion of solids into liquids, and these into gases. The bodies so converted have a great variety of properties. One circumstance common to the cases is the increase of heat. The elimination of other circumstances being complete, this antecedent is rightly assigned as the cause of the change.

Brewster proved that the iridescence of nacre is not due to the nature of the substance, but of the surface. Taking an impression of it in wax, he found on this different substance a like iridescence. It is now a familiar fact that the surface of glass or metal, when finely grooved, becomes iridescent.

If a certain occupation or mode of living is found to be usually attended by a particular disease, it is reasonably suspected to be the cause of the disease; and the exceptional cases wherein the disease does not occur are suspected to involve a preventive cause (§§ 15, 47, 56 n.).

Whenever I eat a particular kind of fruit, whatever else I may eat or drink, however various my general state of health, the temperature of the air, the season, the climate, and divers other surroundings, I am taken ill, and rightly consider the eaten fruit the very probable cause.

A certain plant grows luxuriantly on a certain soil. If wide observation eliminates very generally the other circumstances, it is correct to conclude that soil to be the cause of the remarkable luxuriance of that plant.

If trade languishes or flourishes under a high tariff, and if it be ascertained that those countries where the one effect is observed agree throughout in no other material respect except the tariff, or if this is observed of different decades in the same country, the high tariff may be posited as the cause.

Thus it is by the method of agreement primarily and chiefly that we discern the cause of disease, of political revolution, of national characteristics, of modifications in animal and vegetable physiology, of the order of geological strata, of changes in language; likewise, the effect of storm, of sunshine, and of snow, of good and bad legislation, of this or that method of teaching, of one's habits of life, of æsthetic culture on morals, etc. In short, there is hardly any department of knowledge wherein the method is not in constant use.

§ 64. Some general remarks will now be appropriate. The determination of natural kinds, and in general of phenomena of ultimate coexistence, is by virtue of similarity or agreement (§ 33). The methods of induction by enumeration are also founded on agreement of cases or of marks (§ 37). But the methods now under consideration are not methods of induction, but of inquiry into particular cases of causation. Also they do not apply to ultimately coexisting phenomena, but only to phenomena of succession, and in these only to cases of causal succession.

It is not always easy to determine whether or not successive phenomena are causally connected. Mere succession in time is insufficient (§ 14). The transference of energy is perhaps the ultimate test, but it is rarely applicable (§ 17). We must rely mainly on similar experiences to help us at the outset in distinguishing cases of causation, in separating the causal antecedents from the causal consequents, and in ascertaining the several components of each (§ 35).

In studying a case we disregard the immaterial or chance circumstances. Most instances agree in a number of these. The objects are subject to gravity, immersed in air, exposed to light, etc. Unless these can be supposed to affect the case, they are not taken into account. But no circumstance should be hastily rejected. Light was hardly esteemed an agent until it was detected blackening salts of silver (§ 35); now it is recognized as widely effective in chemical changes and vital processes.

In the distribution of the antecedents and consequents, as well as in their subdivision, care is requisite. Disturbances of the magnetic needle are coincident, more often than chance will account for, with changes on the disk of the sun, and with auroral displays. Hence one of these has been mistaken for the cause of the others, when in fact they are all properly parts of the effect of some widely prevailing common cause.

Among the unquestionable antecedents occur real conditions, which should be distinguished from the causal conditions (§ *110*). Thus joints are a condition, not a cause, of walking. So also molecular mobility is not a cause, but a condition, of crystallization. Again, there are certain doubly refracting (z) substances, Iceland spar being one, having a great variety of color, weight, hardness, form, and composition, which qualities, then, are immaterial circumstances; but solidity, transparency, and in general a crystalline structure, are invariable and essential antecedents, yet not causal conditions (A), but simply real conditions. Such substances exhibit periodical colors on exposure to polarized light, which is a special real, not causal, condition of the periodical colors. The discrimination and elimination of the real conditions are requisite to avoid misleading confusion.

§ 65. Returning to the specific consideration of the method of agreement, we note that after all the foregoing general precautions have been observed, still it is seldom that we have a series of cases either so simple or so complete as the theoretical formula indicates. Usually there is a complex tale of many antecedents and consequents, and it is hard to get the variety of instances requisite to eliminate all save one of the important circumstances attending the phenomenon in question.

Another imperfection in the practical application of this method is called its characteristic imperfection, since it is not attributable to the other methods. An effect given to find its cause is often due to an apparently possible plurality of causes (§ 22). Recurring to the formula (§ 62), it appears, unless the analysis has been thorough, that z may have been in the first instance the effect of B, or of C, in the second of D, in the third of E. Suppose two distinct drugs, each curative of a certain disease, and each mixed with an inert drug; applying the method of agreement we might unguardedly infer the cure to be the effect of the latter.

This difficulty is wholly due to imperfect analysis of facts and factors, and not to any inherent imperfection in the theory. But the best analysis even of the simpler cases is always so far short of perfection that we must admit in practice the maxim of plurality of causes and regard the colligation (§ 9) of results as uncertain.

A multiplication of various instances increases the presumption that A is the cause of z. The error of ascribing the cure to the inert drug would hardly survive even a few cases. Adverting to the first example (§ 63), the possibility that the prismatic colors are the effect in the first instance of the dissolved soap, in the second of the alumina in the mica, in the third of the nitrogen of the air, would soon disappear under additional instances, provided the observations are made amid various circumstances, and the colligated conclusion, that in each instance the colors are the effect of white light on a transparent film constantly present, would soon become a very strong probability, the uncertainty arising from a possible plurality of causes being thereby practically eliminated.

It should be noted that the maxim of a plurality of effects (§ 20) is likewise to be recognized, and the uncertainty thence arising to be similarly reduced by multiplied eliminations. Thus, heat (A) boils water (x), melts metal (y), stimulates growth (s), etc. Elimination of the differences in these effects discovers a common fact (z) in a specific molecular change.

§ 66. It is now sufficiently manifest that in practice a causal connection between a phenomenon and a circumstance cannot be rigidly proved by the method of agreement. A very high degree of probability may sometimes be attained, and with this, when other methods are inapplicable to the case, we have to be content. In most cases the probability is of lower degree, varying in value with the multiplicity of differing instances. A rule for estimating this value is as follows: "Given an effect to be accounted for, and there being several causes that might have produced it, but of whose presence in the particular case nothing is known; the probability that the effect was produced by any of these causes is as the antecedent probability of the cause, multiplied by the probability that the cause, if it existed, would have produced the given effect."[1]

It is also obvious that the method of agreement is a method of simple observation rather than of experiment. When the effect of a given cause is sought, experimental tests are often applicable with advantage (§ 36). When the cause of a given effect is sought, simple observation may give rise only to a suspicion or surmise of the cause; then, reversing the order, the suspected cause may often be tried to see whether z will come of it, which is experimental observation again. But perhaps yet more often the

---

[1] This rule is given by Laplace as the "Sixth Principle," in his "Essai Philosophique sur les Probabilités," and is described by him as the "fundamental principle of that branch of the Analysis of Probabilities which consists in ascending from events to their causes." An excellent exposition, which we have not space to quote, will be found in Mill, *Logic*, p. 385 sq., reproduced by Bain, *Logic*, bk. iii., ch. ix., § 13.

matter is out of reach of handling, and then we are limited to simple observation in both orders of inquiry.

Very generally investigation begins with simple observation by the method of agreement. Recourse is had to experiment if practicable, and the intelligent inquirer will never lose an opportunity of resorting to the more cogent method of difference. Perhaps the chief value of the method of agreement in scientific pursuit is that it suggests lines of experiment, and the application of other methods yielding empirical certainty. In itself it is tentative rather than probative, resulting merely in a greater or less probability that in the observed cases A is the cause of z. Formulæ of the induction may be stated thus:

If A is, then probably z is; and
If z is, then probably A is.

§ 67. An important modification of the foregoing method is the Method of Double Agreement. It consists in applying agreement, first to a series of cases wherein a certain circumstance attends a phenomenon, and then to a series within the same general sphere of circumstances, as nearly similar to the other as possible, except that the phenomenon in question and the attendant circumstance are absent. A comparison of the positive with the negative series greatly strengthens the inference that the phenomenon and the circumstance are causally connected. There is first an agreement in presence, and then an agreement in absence, which double agreement conjoined makes an approach to the conclusiveness of the method of difference.

The argument is: Since the positive cases agree with each other in nothing throughout except in the presence of the given phenomenon and a circumstance, then by the single method of agreement it is probable that these are causally connected. Moreover, since the negative cases agree with each other in nothing throughout except in the absence of the given phenomenon and that circumstance, this, considered apart, likewise renders their connection probable. Therefore, *a fortiori*, the two inferences being conjoined, the connection is still more probable.

The method is stated succinctly in the following CANON OF DOUBLE AGREEMENT: **If instances wherein a phenomenon occurs have only one circumstance in common, and others in which it does not occur have nothing in common save the absence of the circumstance, this wholly or partly is the cause of the phenomenon, or its effect.**

A symbolical formula of this canon is as follows:

$$A\ B\ C \qquad A\ B\ D \qquad A\ C\ F$$
$$a\ b\ c \qquad a\ b\ d \qquad a\ c\ f$$

$$B\ F \qquad C\ D \qquad D\ F$$
$$b\ f \qquad c\ d \qquad d\ f$$

Let it be observed that no negative instance differs from any positive instance merely in the absence of A, a. If one did, it would satisfy the requisites of the simpler, more cogent, and therefore preferable method of difference, and this would supersede the other.

§ 68. In correspondence with the formula, suppose a south wind, Auster, from over a marsh, to be attended by ague in three several instances. In the first, the weather is Bleak and blighting, also Cloudy and cold, but not Damp or Foul. In the second, it is Bleak and blighting, Damp and dewy, but not Cloudy or Foul. In the third, it is Cloudy and cold, Foul and foggy, but not Bleak or Damp. The method of agreement concludes from these cases agreeing in presence that probably the ague was in each caused by Auster charged with malaria from the marsh.

Again, suppose in the same locality another trio of winds not Austral and not attended by ague, but each of the other circumstances appearing in turn in one or two instances, yet no one in all three. The method of agreement infers negatively from these negative cases agreeing in absence that these winds not Austral did not cause ague.

Now this negative inference greatly strengthens the prior conclusion that in those cases the ague was caused by the malarial Auster. For, imagine a series of negative cases exhaustive of the important circumstances associated in any instance with A, a. This series alone would furnish full proof of their causal connection, as follows: Generalizing from a colligation of the negative cases, we have—

If A is not, then a is not; and v.v.;
But in a certain case a is;
∴ In that particular case A is; or v.v.—Tollens.

Practically, however, we can never obtain an exhaustive negative series, hence the conclusion is only probable. But this probability, corroborated by that arising from the affirmative series, yields a conclusion *a fortiori*.

In another important respect the prior conclusion is strengthened still more by the negative series. It excludes the supposition of a plurality of causes. For, since the negative series comprises, theoretically at least, all the antecedents of the affirmative series except A, without the occurrence of a among its consequents, it follows that none of those antecedents is a cause of a. Thus the characteristic imperfection of the method of agreement does not invalidate this modified method, which therefore is the more cogent, and approaches, though it never reaches, the demonstrative force of the method of difference.

§ 69. A standard illustration of the method of double agreement is the research of Wells into the cause of dew. "It appears that the instances in which much dew is deposited, which are very various, agree in this, and, so far as we are able to observe, in this only, that they either radiate heat rapidly or conduct it slowly; qualities between which there is no other circumstance of agreement than that, by virtue of either, the body tends to lose heat from the surface more rapidly than it can be restored from within. The instances, on the contrary, in which no dew, or but a small quantity of it, is formed, and which are also extremely various, agree (as far as we can observe) in nothing except in *not* having this same property. We seem, therefore, to have detected the characteristic difference between the substances on which dew is produced and those on which it is not produced. And thus have been realized the requisitions of what we have termed the Indirect Method of Difference." This, however, is not the whole of the research. By the application of other methods, proof is accumulated, and the theory fully established.[1]

[1] See § 11, last paragraph but one. Mr. Fowler, in his *Inductive Logic*, p. 134, note, says: "Dr. Wells's "Memoir on the Theory of Dew" is very brief, and deserves to be carefully read by every student of scientific method. Sir John Herschel, in his "Discourse," etc., § 168, speaks of the speculation as 'one of the most beautiful specimens of inductive experimental inquiry, lying within a moderate compass,' that is known to him. Cf. *id.*, p. 155. Our quotation is from Mill, *Logic*, p. 299, which is borrowed from Herschel, as above.

IX.—CONCOMITANCE

§ 70. The Method of Concomitant Variations, which may be construed as a modification either of the method of difference or of the method of agreement, remains to be considered.[1] There is a large and important class of cases from which it is impracticable to eliminate entirely an agent and its consequent. To these cases, therefore, neither of the foregoing methods, without modification, is applicable. For instance, the oscillations of a pendulum near a mountain are disturbed; we take it far away, and

---

[1] The method has regard to concomitant changes in the *degree* of a given phenomenon and a circumstance. Observation having noted a gain, or a loss, of quantity in an antecedent and consequent, this gain or loss itself may be taken as a phenomenon and circumstance in which alone this instance differs from another; thus fulfilling the conditions of the method of difference. For example, two observations of a thermometer may discover no difference except a gain of height along with a gain of heat. Or, a series of observations, noting a gain or a loss in each of several instances, may be compared as to this point, in which alone they agree; thus fulfilling the conditions of the method of agreement. For example, observations on mercury, iron, water, and marble, at ordinary temperatures, may agree alone in a loss of bulk along with a loss of heat. The methods, therefore, are primarily two (§ 55).

It will be better, however, to disregard this reduction, and treat the method of concomitant variations as an independent original method.

the disturbance ceases; this proves, by the method of difference, that the mountain was the cause of the disturbance. But we cannot take it away from the earth, and by the same method ascertain the cause of the oscillations. Nor can we apply the method of agreement; for, though the earth, a permanent cause, is always present, so also is the sun, which, by this method alone, might with equal reason be posited as the agent. It is evident that some other method of discovering causal relations is needed. Now, a pendulum oscillates about a vertical through its point of suspension, a vertical whose direction in space varies concomitantly with the earth's motion; therefore the oscillations of the pendulum about the varying vertical, and the moving earth, are causally related.

In general, it follows from the axiom of change (§ 18), that any modified cause, which, indeed, is a different cause, is followed by a modified effect; and any modification of an effect is due to some modification of its cause. Hence, limiting the view to progressive changes attending each other, we have the CANON OF CONCOMITANT VARIATIONS: **If a phenomenon varies in any manner whenever a circumstance varies in some particular manner, they are causally connected.**

Only the general fact of a causal connection can be determined by this method alone. Whether the phenomenon is specifically the cause or the effect of its circumstance, or whether they both are not rather the joint effect ($x \propto x'$) of some common cause, must be ascertained by trying whether we can produce one set of variations, or find one produced, by means of the other. If so, the relation is that of cause and effect, and may be symbolically formulated thus:

$$\begin{array}{ccc} A & B & C \\ 8 & 1 & 1 \\ x & z & y \end{array}$$

Here B with z, and C with y, remain constant, while A varies with x.

§ 71. It is impracticable to deprive a body, a bar of iron for instance, entirely of its heat. We cannot, therefore, so vary the circumstances as to comply with this requisite of the preceding methods, and thus discover what effect is due to the heat. But we can observe a rise of temperature in the bar, and note that the only concurring modification is an increase of bulk, especially of its length. We conclude, by the method of concomitant variations, that its heat and its length are causally connected.

We find, upon trial, that by adding or withdrawing heat we can increase or diminish its length. Hence these are not the joint effect $(x \propto x')$ of some common cause, but are related as cause and effect $(A \propto x)$.

Which is cause of the other? When we increase the heat, the length increases; but when we increase the length by simple traction, the heat does not increase accordingly. When we increase the bulk of some bodies, as air, the temperature, on the contrary, falls. Therefore the varying heat is the cause of the varying length.

This relation being thus particularly ascertained, we are authorized by the principle of uniformity (§ 19) to infer immediately and inductively the general law that heat expands iron, or metals, or bodies.

For further illustration: Sitting in my study, I find myself growing too warm, and observe the thermometer on my table rising. Hence these concomitantly varying phenomena are causally related. But how? The present method, alone applied, does not determine. I suspect, however, from previous experiences, that they are the joint effect of a common cause. On closing the hot-air register the observed variations cease, proving my surmise to be correct.

§ 72. We cite some examples of direct concomitance: On the earth there is no instance of motion persisting indefinitely, and hence the ancients held, by induction from enumeration, that all bodies naturally tend to a state of rest. In proportion, however, as the known obstructions to motion, such as friction, resistance of the air, etc., are abated, the motion is less and less retarded; as in Borda's experiment with the pendulum in a vacuum, the friction at the point of suspension being minimized, the swing continued more than thirty hours. Now, comparing a whole series of cases, from speedy loss of motion to prolonged continuance, we observe that there is a strict concomitance between the degree of obstruction and the retardation. Therefore, it is inferred, if obstruction were wholly removed, the motion would be uniform and perpetual. This proof is given by Newton in support of his induction of the first law of motion (§ 18 n.).

Again, we find that all the variations in the position of the moon are attended by corresponding tidal variations, which is the first step of the process concluding the moon to be the cause determining the tides.

The science of Geology abounds in illustrations. Since the agents with which it is concerned, land and water, subsidence and elevation, denudation and deposition, are constantly present and acting on the earth's surface, it being therefore impossible to eliminate entirely the influence of any one, the geologist, in preparing for an induction explanatory of events long past, is limited very closely to this method.

Also the psycho-physiologist, in seeking to fix the relations between mental powers and cerebral development, also between sensations and neural excitants, since they are inseparable from mind and body at large, has small resource at the outset beyond their concomitant variations.

We cite, also, some examples of inverse concomitance: The apparent size of an object diminishes as the square of its distance increases. Gravity, which varies directly as the mass, varies inversely as the distance squared.

The tendency to chemical action between two substances increases as their cohesion diminishes, being much greater between liquids than between solids.

Mariotte's law, the volume of a gas is in inverse ratio to the pressure, is an induction from observed and measured concomitant variations.

The greater the elevation of the land, the lower the temperature of the climate, and the more scanty the vegetation.

The statistics of crime reveal its general causes. When we find crimes diminishing according as habits of sobriety and industry have increased, according to the multiplication of the means of detection and the more rigorous infliction of penalties, we may presume their causal connection with circumstances that do not admit the method of difference.

§ 73. An important feature of the method still remains to be considered. It will be suitably prefaced by a few general remarks.

The profound and thorough-going distinction between quality and quantity has been emphatically noted (§§ *23, 24, 125 sq.*). A change in a thing that leaves it the same thing which it was—that is, one which does not alter its essence, and so does not amount to a change of kind—is merely an accident, often a change in some respect of degree, of quantity. Sciences are at first merely qualitative, classifying their objects, and treating of their several kinds, but they seek to become also quantitative by measurement of degrees. When they have passed into this latter stage they are more highly esteemed, for then the principles of pure mathematics, the abstract science of quantity, can be applied to their concrete facts, and the knowledge becomes more complete and exact. Astronomy is an illustrious example of a science founded on observation and a few broad inductions, and then developed to extraordinary dimensions, and attaining many new and valuable results by the application of mathematics.

The several methods of discovering the cause or the effect of a given phenomenon, which we have discussed, afford opportunities for passing to a measurement of its quantity which the scientific investigator is eager to use. The qualitative analysis of the chemical laboratory, proceeding mostly and whenever possible by the method of difference, would be comparatively poor in results were it not followed by quantitative analysis. Indeed, alchemy became chemistry just when the balance was introduced for quantitative estimates. In the earlier part of this century most of the phenomena of electricity and magnetism were known and classified merely as facts; now they can for the most part be measured and calculated. The attempt is making to subject even mental phenomena to measurement, and by the determination of their relative quantities to raise psychology to the rank of an exact science. The effort to bring logic under the dominion of mathematics has been noticed (§ 74). The result is a purely artificial structure, as truly so as the calculus of a fourth dimension, or the geometry of curved space—ingenious and curious, but without any corresponding reality. Such speculation is practically useless and misleading, and is mentioned here merely to indicate the strong tendency of scientists to apply measurement and mathematical form to all branches of knowledge.

§ 74. We have examined applications of the method of concomitant variations to cases that cannot be resolved by the other methods. But it has very important applications in connection with these. Especially is it of inestimable importance in determining comparative quantities. After a causal relation has been ascertained by other methods, this one is often applied in determining the ratio of the cause and effect. Recurring to a previous example (§ 61), when by the method of residue it was definitely ascertained that the passage of light requires time, then the variations of the time concomitant with those of the distance furnished Roemer with data for calculating its velocity.

But apart from other methods, this one often leads to an important measure of quantity. The velocity of a body falling freely varies concomitantly with the distance fallen. This is an easy observation. The exact ratio of the increase of distance and the increase of velocity is not so readily ascertained, but Atwood's machine determines it to be as 1, 2, 3 - - - - to 1, 3, 5 - - - -. It also determines the absolute quantity of fall from rest in the first second to be 16.08 feet. From these data can be calculated its fall during any subsequent second, and its acquired velocity at any point of its fall.

The respective action of the sun and moon in producing the tides may be estimated quantitatively from the varying positions of those two bodies.

These examples are sufficient to indicate the important part the method of concomitant variations plays in the progress of a science, especially in facilitating its passage into an advanced stage, and its further development under the sway of mathematics.

§ 75. In making a quantitative induction from measured variations—that is, in applying mathematical results deduced from observed cases to cases beyond experience—provision is to be had on at least three points.

First, we should know the absolute quantities of both A and x, as well as their relative variation. For, if we cannot fix the total quantity of each, we cannot fix a thorough-going ratio. Not only must A and x, or x and x', vary concomitantly—they must also vanish together. Because heat expands a body, we cannot infer that the distance between its particles is due wholly to heat, so that, if all heat were withdrawn, they would be in contact; for we do not know the amount of heat in a body,[1] or the distance between its particles, and hence cannot know whether the two would vanish simultaneously. But in the case of a falling body, cited above, we have the absolute zero both of the distance fallen, the starting-point, and of the velocity, the state of rest

---

[1] The thermal zero has not been observed, but by calculation has been fixed at $-273°$ C., or $-459°$ F.

from which it falls, and are consequently justified in fixing their ratio.

Second, in general we cannot be sure that beyond the limit of observation there may not develop some modifying agent, latent in the observed circumstances, which will falsify our induction. The induction that heat expands bodies (§ 71) is subject, even in this inexact form of statement, to a number of exceptions. Yet more emerge when the degree of expansion and contraction is measured and inductively posited. Indeed, the contrary sometimes occurs. Water at ordinary temperatures expands as it warms, and contracts as it cools, but when cooled below 39° it begins and continues to expand until it becomes ice at 32°, which is supposed by Grove to be due to the setting in of crystallization.

Third, when the observed variations are within narrow limits, a very small error in the estimate may, beyond those limits, enlarge in geometrical ratio. This occasion for uncertainty, unlike the preceding, is peculiar to the method of concomitant variations. It is very hazardous, for example, to extend an ascertained ratio of expansion and temperature— that is, the numerical coefficient of expansion—far beyond the limits of observation. By being thus extended the early formulas for the elasticity of steam have led to disaster.[1] So we can be sure of

---

[1] "The formulæ," says Sir John Herschel, "Discourse," etc., § 187, "which have been empirically deduced for the elasticity of steam (till very recently), and those for the resistance of fluids, and other similar subjects, have almost invariably failed to support the theoretical

our induction only when it does not greatly exceed the extreme limits that have been subjected to observation and measurement.

structures which have been erected on them." Mr. Mill adds: "... when relied on beyond the limits of the observations from which they were deduced."—*Logic*, p. 291.

X.—DEDUCTION

§ 76. In the syllogism a general proposition is premised, from which is inferred a conclusion of equal or less generality, or a particular individual fact (§ 3).

The general proposition may be an intuitive primary axiom, or an inference from axioms. In either of these cases the process is wholly deductive and strictly demonstrative or apodictic, as in pure mathematics, and in the logic of forms. With it the present treatise has no concern save to point out that the formal theorems of induction, and of its preparatory steps, are deductions from axioms.

Otherwise the general proposition premised is an induction, from which a deduction is made by subsuming some subsidiary truth. The great body of reasoning in the so-called inductive sciences, and in the practical affairs of life, is of this character. Hence a treatise on logic limited to a discussion of the Aristotelic deductive processes is essentially incomplete; and, on the other hand, the notion, which has widely prevailed, that induction is capable of advantageously superseding deduction, and alone is worthy of consideration, arises from an entire misconception of the nature and several ends of the two processes, and of their essentially complementary relation.[1]

[1] The Logic of Aristotle received the title ὄργανον, not from himself, but from his followers. It is clear that he did not regard it as an organon, an aid or instrument of discovery, but as a propœdeutic.—See *Meta.*, iv., 3 (1005 b. 4). The title came into general use in the fifteenth century.—See St. Hilaire, *De la Logique d'Aristote*, tom. i., p. 19. Bacon's second book of the "Instauratio Magna" is entitled "Novum Organum" (1620), and is evidently intended to elaborate an instrument of discovery. Dr. Whewell, dissatisfied with its methods, gives us his "Novum Organon Renovatum."

The designation "Organon" has led to much error. For two centuries after Bacon it was commonly held that his was a new method, superseding the effete method of Aristotle. But in the last half-century a better understanding has come to prevail. Deduction and Induction together constitute Logic, and Logic in both branches is merely "an analysis and systematic exposition of what we are all doing from morning till night, and continue to do even in our dreams" (Macaulay, *Essay on Bacon*). In support of our view of the relation of Deduction and Induction, we quote the following authorities:

Aristotle says: "All learning is derived from things previously known, as we also stated in the Analytics; and is derived partly from induction [δἰ ἐπαγωγῆς], and partly from syllogism. Now, induction is the origin of the universal; but a syllogism is deduced from universals. There are, therefore, some principles from which the syllogism is deduced, which are not themselves syllogistically established; they are therefore established by induction."—*Nic. Eth.*, vi., 3 (3); cf. *ibid.*, vi., 8 (9); *Meta.*, i., 1; *Post. Anal.*, ii., 19. Also see Grote, *Aristotle*, ch. vi., p. 276 sq.

Sir John Herschel says: "It is to our immortal countryman, Bacon, that we owe the broad announcement of this grand and fertile principle, and the development of the idea that the whole of natural philosophy consists entirely of a series of inductive generalizations, commencing with the most circumstantially stated particulars, and carried up to universal laws or axioms, which comprehend in their statements every subordinate degree of generality; and of a corresponding series of inverted reasoning from generals to particulars, by which these axioms are traced back to their remotest consequences, and all par-

In the preceding exposition of the several methods of observation and experiment by which we contrive to distinguish among a mass of coexistent phenomena the particular effect due to a given cause,

ticular propositions deduced from them; as well those by whose immediate consideration we rose to their discovery, as those of which we had no previous knowledge."—*Discourse, etc.*, ch. iii., § 96. This passage, which Dr. Whewell prefixes as a motto to his "Nov. Org. Renov.," reminds us that Buckle, in his "Essay on Induction," says that Induction is inference from a reality to an idea, and Deduction is inference from an idea to a reality.

Sir William Hamilton says: "The deductive and inductive processes are elements of Logic equally essential. Each requires the other. The former is only possible through the latter; the latter is valuable only as realizing the possibility of the former. As our knowledge commences with the apprehension of singulars, every *class* or *universal whole* is consequently only a knowledge *at second hand*. Deductive reasoning is thus not an original and independent process. The universal major proposition, out of which it develops the conclusion, is itself [if not an axiom] necessarily the conclusion of a foregone induction, and mediately [?] or immediately, an inference, a collection, from individual objects of perception or self-consciousness. Logic, therefore, as a definite and self-sufficient science, must equally vindicate the *formal* purity of the synthetic illation by which it ascends to its wholes, as of the analytic illation by which it re-descends to their parts.—*Discussions*, p. 160 (Harper's ed.). See, also, *id.*, p. 157 sq. Cf. *Metaphysics*, Lec. vi.

Mr. J. S. Mill says: "We shall, conformably to usage, consider the name Induction as belonging to the process of establishing the general proposition, and the remaining operation we shall call by its usual name, Deduction. And we shall consider every process, by which anything is inferred respecting an unobserved case, as consisting of an Induction followed by a Deduction; because, although the process need not necessarily be carried on in this form, it is always susceptible of the form, and must be thrown into it when assurance of scientific accuracy is needed and desired."—*Logic*, p. 154. Cf. Venn, *Empirical Logic*, ch. xiv., p. 363 sq.

or the particular cause which gave birth to a given effect, it has been repeatedly indicated that, the relation being first definitely ascertained in a particular case or cases, the axioms of uniformity authorize a generalization extending to unknown cases—that is, an induction of all possible like cases under a universal proposition or law. Also it has been stated that such propositions serve as major premises, from which to make deductions (§§ 32, 59). This is specifically proof, often resulting in discovery. A new case being brought under the general proposition, and a conclusion proved respecting it, this conclusion, if previously unknown, is a discovery.

The induction *All matter gravitates* has been made, we will suppose for illustration, from observations on solids and liquids. Now do gases gravitate? We have only to establish *All gases are matter*, in order to deduce *All gases gravitate*, or *have weight*. This, in form, is not a mere find, but a scientific investigation and discovery.

Again, suppose we have *All celestial objects showing a proper motion among the stars, and shining with reflected light, are planets of the solar system.* We descry a telescopic object, seen by reflection, and having a proper motion, and discover it to be a planet. If, furthermore, its path is found to lie between the orbits of Mars and Jupiter, we have discovered another one of the many asteroids.

The research into the cause of dew (§ 69) led to the establishment of an inductive generalization, from which deductions were made to cases theretofore unexplained, thus resulting in a discovery of the true cause of certain phenomena, such as the "sweating" of a pitcher of iced water.

Note that the minor in the first example is a universal. It is not, however, an induction, but merely the result of identification under definition (§ 10). Matter is defined as extended and impenetrable, which, being found true of gases, gives the proposition *Gases are matter*. Questions of identity to establish a minor are a necessary part of research, but should not be mistaken for inductive inquiries establishing a major. Are alloys definite chemical compounds, or mere mixtures, is a question of identity under definition.

When a deduction to an unobserved fact has been made, it remains to verify the conclusion. This is to seek for and observe a particular instance, either one occurring naturally, or one produced artificially. Having inferred that *Gases gravitate*, we exhaust a vessel of its air, and find that it loses weight. By the method of difference we rightly judge the weight lost to be that of the withdrawn air. This verifies our inference, and also strengthens the premised induction.[1]

Deduction thus normally subsequent to induction often leads to further induction, as in the method of residue (§ 60), and in other preparatory processes.

---

[1] It will be seen, by the foregoing exposition of the general relations of induction and deduction, that, in logical order, the order of thought and investigation, induction comes first. In didactic order, deduction usually comes first.

But deduction has a specific application in the investigation of certain causal relations which calls for detailed consideration.

§ 77. There are two kinds of effect which must be set clearly apart. The distinction is very important, and runs deep, being due to the ultimate nature of things. An effect of one kind has properties quite different from those of the effect of any of its antecedents operating apart from the others. Thus, oxygen and hydrogen unite to form water; but in water not a trace of the effective properties of either factor is discernible. Hence it is impossible to deduce from such factors the consequent of their conjoint action. To ascertain it an observation of the product is requisite, which observation may often be verified, not merely by direct experiment, but by an inverse process of analyzing the product into its originating components. This kind of effect is aptly termed heterogeneous or heteropathic, the conjoint effect differing in kind from those separately produced. It is also called chemical, because the clearest and most abundant examples are to be found in chemical actions; as, the taste of sugar of lead is wholly unlike that of acetic acid or any other of its components, and the color of blue vitriol is neither that of copper nor of sulphuric acid. There is, in short, a change of properties so nearly complete that the effect cannot be predicted from the given cause, nor indeed the cause from the given effect.[1] It is to

[1] To this change of properties weight at least has been accounted an

the resolution of this class of cases that the foregoing methods are especially adapted.

An effect of the other kind has properties quite similar to those of the effects of its antecedents operating separately. When two simultaneous impulses, which may differ in direction and intensity, impart motion to a body, the resultant motion is an effect quite similar to the effects which the impulses acting successively would produce, and the terminal result is identical.[1] Hence it is possible to deduce from such factors the consequent of their conjoint action without observing it. The inference may often be verified by direct observation of a case, but not by any reverting analysis of the product, such analysis being impracticable. This kind of effect is termed homogeneous, as of like kind to those separately produced. It is also called mechanical, since its clearest and most abundant examples are to be found in mechanics, both terrestrial and celestial. In general, it is a composition of forces or causes, giving an intermixture of effects, a homogeneous result not susceptible of analysis into its originating components.[2]

exception; for the weight of any composite substance whatever is always precisely the sum of the weights of its components. This it is that has made the science of Chemistry possible (§ 18, note, and § 73). But weight is not truly an exception to the foregoing statements, since it is not properly a chemical but a mechanical property, not a molecular but a molar activity.

[1] See Newton's second law of motion, § 18, note.

[2] This composition of causes or intermixture of effects is liable to be confused with plurality of causes (§ 22). In both a number of

Cases of a homogeneous intermixture of effects are very much more common than those of the other class. Indeed, they abound on every hand, and in all departments of knowledge. A lake is fed by rains and rivers, but no examination of the lake will tell how much is due to each. Wind often concurs with tide to make high water. The moon's orbit is a resultant of attracting and tangential forces, centripetal and centrifugal. A good crop is a single effect; the agency, multiple. An invalid plies all means to regain health; many influences combine, but the effect is indivisible. A voluntary effort is the offspring of many feelings. The rise and fall of prices, the general prosperity of a country, and the increase of population seldom depend on a single cause, yet the effect is homogeneous.

§ 78. Let us examine these two classes of causal relation, first with reference to the problem given cause to find effect, reserving the inverse for treatment in the next following chapter.

As to the class marked by a heterogeneous effect, since we can infer nothing from the properties of the antecedents respecting the character of the consequent, we are shut up to the methods of investiga-

---

antecedents is involved; but in the latter there is a plurality of distinct causes, to either of which the effect may apparently be due, and we are at loss to fix on the true one; whereas in the former there is a plurality of co-operating antecedents, each of which, producing a special effect when alone, produces the same when acting conjointly with the others, and we are at loss to assign to each its due share.

tion which have already been discussed. These are based on simple observation of facts or on experiment, and the procedure is *a posteriori* by elimination.

As to the class marked by a homogeneous effect, that is, a composition of causes yielding an intermixture of effects, since the consequent is not susceptible of analysis into its actual constituents, none of the foregoing methods is competent to cope with it; for those methods, proceeding essentially by elimination, require, in order to this, an analysis, a discrimination of the constituent facts of both antecedent and consequent. This, as to the consequent, being impracticable, the preceding methods fail. If $A\ B\ C$ are followed, not by $y\ z\ x$, but by a; and if $B\ C$ still produce a, nothing is eliminated from the consequent, and no point is gained.[1]

We are obliged, therefore, in case of a homogeneous effect, to seek some other method of investigation. The homogeneity of the effect furnishes ground for an inference from the effects of the

---

[1] In some exceptional cases, however, the preceding methods yield results. If A and a vary together, they are causally connected; and if with the total disappearance of A there is a loss of $\frac{1}{4}a$, this proves by the methods of concomitance and difference that A causes $\frac{1}{4}a$. If, as the weather becomes warmer, one's appetite diminishes, he may be pretty sure that the appetite is affected by the season, though other facts co-operate. Dr. Parkes ascertained that a muscle grows during exercise, and loses bulk during rest; but there are other causes of its growth. If a floating glass globe loses $\frac{1}{10}$ of its displacement on being exhausted of air, this is proof that the weight of the contained air caused that much of the displacement.

causes acting apart to the effect of their conjoint action. This presupposes the ascertainment, by some of the preceding methods, of the particular effect of each of the given causes, and generally an induction of the law according to which each cause operates. Then we proceed *a priori* to deduce their conjoint effect, either from the inductions themselves or from their several consequences. Thus we have a new distinct method, which, since it proceeds by deduction, is called the Deductive Method.[1]

The problem to be solved by the deductive method is, to find the composite effect from the laws of the several composing causes. The logical form of the procedure is concisely expressed in the following Canon of Deduction: **If from the several laws of a plurality of co-operating antecedents a composite consequent be deduced, this will be the conjoint effect of the antecedents.**

The method may be formally illustrated as follows: Let x be the unknown total. Now—

If from A can be inferred $\frac{1}{6}x$,
and from B "   "   " $\frac{2}{3}x$,
and from C "   "   " $\frac{1}{2}x$,
and from D "   "   " $-\frac{1}{3}x$,

then their algebraic sum is the conjoint effect x.

For an example of a particular case, suppose we wish to find the velocity of a train of cars at the foot of a grade. If we can ascertain that the initial pro-

---

[1] The name is not felicitous, seeing that it is not sharply distinctive, and hence tends to confusion; but, having been generally adopted by logical writers, it is here retained.

pulsion causes a velocity of 10 feet a second, the pull of the engine while running down 40, gravity 30, and that friction causes a retardation of 20, then the sum of the several velocities thus ascertained is its final velocity. If, now, we actually measure the final velocity and find it the same as that calculated, our estimate is thereby verified. Theoretically this is a very simple case, practically it would be difficult.[1] Yet this method is the sole one applicable to it, and to a great variety of cases, many of great intricacy; nevertheless it has often led to very brilliant results.

§ 79. The deductive method, including its prepparation and confirmation, may be viewed as consisting of three several stages.

1st. Induction.[2] This, the causes having been separately investigated, makes induction of their several laws. Many celestial phenomena remained unexplained until the mechanical laws of certain causes, especially the laws of motion (§ 18 n.), were ascertained and furnished a basis for explanation.

[1] Often forces are in equilibrium, as in mechanical action and reaction producing rest (§ 18, note, 3d law). If A produces a, and B produces $-a$, the causes neutralizing each other as to any perceptible change, we may have no suspicion that they are in operation at all. Thus an equal balance at rest gives no sign of the downward forces in play. Rest is the effect produced, and the forces must be described, in terms of pressure, by their tendency to produce motion (§ 52).

[2] The first stage is called induction because there must be an induction as the basis of the whole. In many particular investigations the place of the induction may be supplied by a prior deduction, but the ultimate major premise of the prior deduction must have been obtained by induction.

If the subject be a social phenomenon, the premises prerequisite to its determination are certain laws of human action, and certain properties of outward things by which the conduct of men in society is influenced. Thus certain political and social antecedents are regarded as explanatory of the French Revolution.

2d. Deduction. This infers from the laws of the causes their combined effect. If the cases subsumed be general, the conclusions will be general. If they be particular, so will the conclusions be; as, the predicted positions of the planets, found in the nautical almanac. When the terms of the premises have been subjected to quantitative measurement (§ 73), the deduction becomes a process of mathematical calculation. To determine the path of a projectile, a cannon-ball for instance, the causes which affect its range and velocity must first be known and measured; as, the force of the powder, the action of gravity, the angle of elevation, the resistance of the air, the force and direction of the wind. The laws of these being given, and particular cases subsumed, still it is a very difficult mathematical problem so to combine the results as to deduce the effect of their collective action.

3d. Verification. This tests the conclusion by comparing it with actual fact. If these agree, the conclusion is confirmed. The function of verification is not proof, but merely the confirmation of proof. Still its value is inestimable, and it cannot be dispensed with. In numerous and important cases the agencies are so many and various, often more or less counteracting one another, that we can hardly ever be sure that we have taken all into account, or have estimated rightly those that we know. Moreover, when these conditions are fairly fulfilled, to make the computation in any but very simple cases transcends our calculus. Witness the unsolved problem of three gravitating bodies. Save in rare instances our results are at best only approximations. To warrant reliance on the conclusion, it must be found to accord with a direct observation of the inferred facts, or with an empirical generalization of them. Should a discrepancy between the inference and the observation appear, it will lead to a correction of error, or be indicative of some unnoticed residue, which may lead to additional discovery (§ 60).

In Newton's procedure that establishes the identity of terrestrial gravity with the force that deflects the moon's motion, or, in other words, that proves the attraction of the earth to be the cause of the deflection, all three of the foregoing stages occur.[1]

[1] The statement that follows is quoted from Mill, *Logic*, p. 350. It should be noted that the order of procedure indicated here, and indeed throughout this treatise, is the logical order. The historical order—that is, the actual order of the thoughts of an investigator—is very various, anticipating, reverting, passing to and fro over the whole ground; dwelling now on this point, now on that, overleaping necessary means; returning to finish the unfinished, making excursions into collateral regions, etc., so that it would perhaps be impossible for him to record his actual procedure. But the logical order of statement links all in a continuous chain of reason and consequent, and may be regarded as a corrected restatement of the process.

"First, it is proved from the moon's motions that the earth attracts her with a force varying as the inverse square of the distance. This, though partly dependent on prior deductions, corresponds to the first or purely inductive step, the ascertainment of the law of the cause (§ 89).

"Secondly, from this law, and from the knowledge previously obtained of the moon's mean distance from the earth, and of the actual amount of her deflection from the tangent, it is ascertained with what rapidity the earth's attraction would cause the moon to fall, if she were no farther off, and no more acted upon by extraneous forces, than terrestrial bodies are. That is the second step, the ratiocination.

"Finally, this calculated velocity being compared with the observed velocity with which all heavy bodies fall, by mere gravity, towards the surface of the earth (§ 74), the two quantities are found to agree." The proof is thus perfected, the identity established, the cause of the deflection ascertained with physical certainty to be the attraction of the earth. The logical process is complete in all its parts.

XI.—HYPOTHESIS

§ 80. When a novel phenomenon occurs which cannot at once be referred to its kind or otherwise explained, we are perplexed and dissatisfied. This prompts us to assign it provisionally to some known class or cause to which we suppose it may belong. If the matter be trifling, we are usually satisfied by a guess, and dismiss it. If it be important, we follow the clew implied in the guess, and investigate the case until perhaps a plausible supposition is reached. Closer investigation may lead to knowledge, but very often we cannot get beyond a suspicion, a good guess, a fair conjecture, a reasonable supposition, or at best a probable assumption.

Whoever will attentively consider his own mental operations will find that almost always they thus consist at the outset of suppositions, that these guide his inquiries, and that very often he is unable to pass beyond to positive knowledge, but must rest content with probability. He will find, not only that his thoughts are constantly employed with suppositions, and that they comprise the great body of his most mature reflections, but also that without the aid of these as percursors it would hardly be possible to attain any satisfactory knowledge of anything whatever.

A supposition or hypothesis has the form of a representative idea—a mental image of what is at least logically possible. The making it is the work chiefly of the reflective or the practical imagination, the thinking faculty co-operating and restraining.[1] That the earth is even now a sphere of molten fluid intensely hot, enclosed by a thin crust comparable to an egg-shell, is an hypothesis that required a bold imagination to frame, and requiring, we may add, a like imagination to comprehend. A special vigor of this faculty, disciplined by thought, is characteristic of discoverers in science and of inventors in the arts. By it they make tentative excursions into unexplored regions, increasing and utilizing knowledge.

The methodical use of suppositions in trifles is precisely the same as in the noblest sciences. One cannot hear a knock at his door, or see a flash, or smell an odor, or feel a pain, without instantly, almost instinctively, making a supposition to explain it. Questions in common talk conform to suppositions in mind. Tares appear among the wheat; good seed was sown; whence come the tares? An enemy hath done this. The plausible supposition may be rendered highly probable by circumstantial evidence, as the courts call it, against the accused, who, while enjoying the presumption of innocence, is tried on

---

[1] These mental relations are more fully stated with illustrations in *Psychology*, §§ 200, 202, 214.

the supposition of guilt. This, unless established by direct evidence, remains a supposition—that is, an unproved proposition—only becoming more or less probable according to the circumstances. Yet, if it be shown that no other supposition can be maintained, this is proof, legal and logical.[1] We have passed from trifles into serious matter. Now, if we turn to the great sciences that solve the mysteries of nature, or to theology that tells us of God, we shall find the same logical principles and processes, the same use of conjecture, supposition, and hypothesis, in the course through which the loftiest truth is attained. It is the province of logic in general to disclose and formulate the natural processes of thinking, and in particular to unfold in this place the important part played by hypothesis.[2]

---

[1] "Let any one watch the manner in which he himself unravels a complicated mass of evidence; let him observe how, for instance, he elicits the true history of any occurrence from the involved statements of one or of many witnesses; he will find that he does not take all the items of evidence into his mind at once, and attempt to weave them together; he extemporizes, from a few of the particulars, a first rude theory [supposition, hypothesis] of the mode in which the facts took place, and then looks at the other statements one by one, to try whether they can be reconciled with that provisional theory [hypothesis], or what alterations or additions it requires to make it square with them. In this way we arrive, by means of hypotheses, at conclusions not hypothetical."—Mill, *Logic*, p. 354.

[2] A thesis (Gr.) is a proposition posited (Lat.); an hypothesis is one supposited or supposed. The words hypothesis and supposition have thus a like etymology, and are synonyms. The latter in usage is applied more freely to commonplace and transient notions; the former to such as are scientific and settled, and so has rather more dignity.

§ 81. The various methods of investigating to ascertain the causal relation between a given phenomenon and its circumstances involve necessarily a constant use of suppositions. When an effect is given to find its cause, we are limited to simple observation, and seek for a natural occurrence of an instance wherein the antecedents can be noted. When one has been found, the first step is to reject the immaterial circumstances, and then to distribute the remainder into antecedents and consequents. Now, it is quite obvious that even this much cannot be done, unless there be in the mind of the observer some idea, however vague and unsettled, of the cause he is seeking, some suggestion from experience of analogous cases, some clew, some index, some surmise, conjecture, supposition, to guide him in a tentative application of one or another of the methods of investigation. This is essential to any intelligent observation, which otherwise would be no more than the stupid gazing of a boor. The supposition, arising perhaps in a very loose and uncertain way, may soon prove quite erroneous and be rejected, whereby a negative point is gained. Another takes its place, and investigation is renewed, guided constantly by a supposition. Illustrations of this mode of research are seen in the various hypotheses on the nature of comets and nebulæ. Others may be taken from various literary hypotheses which have laid claim to acceptance; as, the hypothesis of Wolf respecting the origin of the Homeric poems; that of Niebuhr, deriving the stories of early Rome from lost ballads or epics; those of Eichhorn, Marsh, and others concerning the origin of the text of the Gospels; the many concerning the authorship of the Œconomics attributed to Aristotle, and of the Letters of Junius. In such cases suppositions are made, and then supported by circumstantial evidence. The form of logical procedure in the grave matter of scripture exegesis, or, generally, in the interpretation of language, is quite similar.[1]

It is equally obvious that all experimental observation is likewise dependent on supposition. A mere trial of possible combinations to see what will come of them, without the further suggestions of a suggested supposition, can elicit nothing, save by chance. Indeed, that cannot properly be called an experiment which does not proceed upon some tolerably well defined hypothesis. Cavendish, suspecting that water is not an element, was led by positive supposition to burn hydrogen with oxygen, and thus discovered its composition. Davy, conjecturing the alkalies to be metallic oxides, and following a clew suggested by analogy, proved it on decomposing them in a galvanic circuit. Franklin sailed his kite on a surmise of the identity of lightning with the electricity of his machine. Bacon stuffed a dressed fowl with snow, to test his supposition that cold would keep meat sweet. Columbus sailed westward on the hypothesis

---

[1] A striking example of the application of the hypothetical deductive method to interpretation is the deciphering, by Champollion, in 1822, of the famous Rosetta stone, whereby the Egyptian alphabet was discovered.

that the earth is round, and hence that he could thus reach the Indies. Socialists attempt revolution, and legislators enact tentative laws on hypothetical grounds. Whenever anybody tries to do any new thing with the least modicum of intelligence, he is trying to realize a suppositive idea, and no scientific procedure of any sort is possible unless in accord with a preconceived hypothesis.

§ 82. A more formal use of hypothesis—one more generally recognized by logicians and scientists—is now to be examined at some length.

In the previous chapter, of which this is a continuation, it was shown that the law of each of several given causes, which together produce a homogeneous effect, being inductively ascertained, we may, in simple cases, deduce their united effect, and then verify this result by comparing it with observed fact. We thus determine the effect to be expected in certain cases wherein the several co-operating causes intermixing their effects are known. The logical order of the whole procedure is, first induction, then deduction, then verification. This is the deductive method as applied to solve the problem: Given a certain composition of causes, to find what homogeneous effect will follow (§ 78). We have now to show how the deductive method is applied to solve the inverse problem: Given a homogeneous effect, to find the cause or causes producing it, or their laws.

It is quite evident that, owing to the homogeneity

of a mechanical effect, an analysis of it into its components is impracticable, and therefore no direct application of this or any of the preceding methods will solve the present problem. The obstacle may also be explained as due to the quasi-principle of a plurality of causes (§ 22). Referring to the illustration drawn from the composition of motion, it is evident that, given the motion of a body, no practicable analysis of this effect, which is but a part, though the chief one, of the consequents, will enable us to determine what force or forces were its actual cause; since there is an infinite number of combinations of impulses, varying in intensity and direction, which might have produced precisely this partial effect. To find hypothetically, for instance, what impelling force or forces, with their point of application, direction, and intensity, might have produced the existing projectile and rotary motion of the earth, is an easy problem; but to ascertain what combination of impulses, if any, did actually produce it, is impossible from any data we possess.

The difficulty is not always so absolutely insuperable. There are many and very important cases, in which an indirect application of the deductive method attains, by the aid of hypothesis, results of inestimable scientific value. It consists in substituting for the induction of the first stage of the direct deductive method (§ 79), an hypothesis of the cause or of its law, and then proceeding as before, the stages now being, first hypothesis, then deduction, then verification. This modified application of the deductive method, we shall now examine more particularly.[1]

§ 83. Let us first define the term. In its most general sense, an hypothesis is an unproved, and may be an unprovable, proposition. More specifically, it is a proposition laid down, without evidence or with insufficient evidence, from which to draw conclusions relative to facts, under the notion that, if the conclusions are in accord with known facts, the hypothesis either is, or is likely to be, true.[2] In undertaking to explain the formal use of scientific hypothesis, we venture this yet more restricted definition: **A scientific hypothesis is an ideal assumption of a cause or law.**

§ 84. For many cases of a mechanical effect whose cause is unknown, a known cause, with its known law, is hypothetically posited; from this supposition a deduction is made, and its conclusion verified by observation. Thus it has frequently occurred to a scattered cluster of powder-magazines that when one is exploded the others immediately explode. How shall we account for or what causes this uni-

[1] Comte puts the process in a sentence, saying: "Some fact is as yet little understood, or some law is unknown; we frame on the subject an hypothesis as accordant as possible with the whole of the data already possessed; and the science, being thus enabled to move forward freely, always ends by leading to new consequences capable of observation, which either confirm or refute, unequivocally, the first supposition."—*Philosophie Positive*, tom. ii., p. 434.

[2] See Mill, *Logic*, p. 249; and Bain, *Logic*, bk. iii., ch. 13.

formity? The hypothesis has been assumed that aerial vibrations, whose mode of motion and of communicating motion are well known, are the cause. Now, if in general aerial vibrations can cause explosion, it is deductively inferred that intense explosives, as cordite, nitrogen iodide, or fulminate of mercury, shall readily be exploded by the vibrations which a similar explosion produces, or even by a musical note. Experiments have verified this conclusion, thus rendering the hypothesis probable.

Let it be remarked that in this case the cause hypothetically posited is a *vera causa*—that is, one known in other connections to be a cause.[1] So we may assume the cause of an epidemic to be excessive heat, or bad drainage, or imported bacteria, each being a *vera causa*, and push the inquiry accordingly. The glacial hypothesis, accounting for the character and distribution of erratic boulders, assigns the observed action of glaciers and ice-floes as the cause; and the science of geology in general, finding in the earth's crust strata and masses of rock quite similar to observed deposits from water and products of volcanic fire, assumes these *veræ causæ* as explanatory of those ancient formations.

[1] The phrase *vera causa* is taken from Newton's first Rule of Philosophizing (§ 21 n.). His meaning seems plain enough when we consider that he was proposing gravity, a cause known to operate near the earth, as the cause of planetary motions, to take the place of the ideal vortices of Descartes, in the theory of celestial mechanics. Still the phrase has been much discussed, and variously interpreted. See Herschel, *Discourse, etc.*, § 137 sq.; Whewell, *Phil. of Dis.*, ch. xviii., § 7 sq.; Mill, *Logic*, p. 353.

It is not, however, as has been claimed, essential in scientific investigation that the cause assumed shall be a *vera causa*, but such assumption brings the case nearer to and facilitates complete proof, and hence is the most promising form of this general mode of inquiry.¹ There is, indeed, no other limit to hypothesis than that of imagination; but natural science admits only such hypothetical agencies as are allied, at least by analogy, with known causes and laws in nature. The assumption of a supernatural cause to account for a natural event is unscientific, and characteristic of superstition; as, to attribute an epidemic to the ill-will of a witch, or table-rappings to spirits.

In illustration of a cause wholly hypothetical—that is, one not a *vera causa*, but invented and supposed—we cite the undulatory hypothesis of light originally proposed by Huyghens. This assumes space to be filled with an ether whose vibrations, according with the known laws of vibration in elastic fluids, account for many of the phenomena of light. The supposition has given unity to the science of light, and served as an excellent working hypothesis; but independent evidence of the real existence of such an ether is still lacking, though it has been earnestly sought, especially in watching for a retardation of the motion of comets attributable only to a resisting

---

¹ "Any hypothesis which has so much plausibility as to explain a considerable number of facts, helps us to digest these facts in proper order, to bring new ones to light, and make *experimenta crucis* for the sake of future inquiries."—Hartley, *Obs. on Man*, vol. i., p. 16.

medium. The assumed cause, then, is not a *vera causa*, and until it be proved to be one, it is not strictly proper to speak even of this most admirable and truly scientific hypothesis as a theory.[1]

§ 85. Instead of a hypothetical cause acting according to known law, there may be posited a known cause acting according to hypothetical law. For instance, the kinetic hypothesis of gases assumes that their mechanical properties are due to a peculiar mode of activity of the molecules. This activity of the known cause is supposed to be in accordance with the laws of motion, inertia and others, which, since they are known to be true laws in other relations, *veræ leges*, correspond in this hypothesis to the *veræ causæ* in those just discussed. The gaseous molecules are represented as constantly moving with great velocity, those of hydrogen at zero having a rate of one and one-seventh miles a second; also as colliding with each other, and impinging on the sides of a containing vessel, which expenditure of *vis viva* is the pressure of the gas. As the temperature rises, the molecules move faster, strike harder and oftener, and the pressure is greater. It is their great and incessant molecular activity that causes the expansion and diffusion of gases, to which is due the uniformity

---

[1] The terms theory and hypothesis should not be used indifferently. Hypothesis is the more general term including mere conjecture. Theory is hypothesis of only the highest order, grounded on a *vera causa*, and systematically elaborated. Moreover, after complete proof, the theorem, though no longer hypothetical, is still called a theory.

of our mixed atmosphere. This hypothesis of a peculiar mode or law of activity has been developed mathematically, and deductions made from it have been verified. It is accepted by many physicists.

There are also instances in science wherein hypothesis has respect both to the cause and to its law. The development hypothesis, proposing to account for the origin of species, was announced, in crude form, five centuries before the Christian era, and has never been entirely abandoned. What Mr. Darwin did for it was to amplify and perfect the hypothesis of the causes, environment, use and disuse, and heredity, showing that they are *veræ causæ*, then to postulate the law of natural selection or the survival of the fittest, and show it to be a *vera lex* under which fairly permanent changes of type in both fauna and flora are actually effected, this being also a verification. Still, his famous speculation, serving as an excellent guide of work, and remodelling all branches of natural history, remains an hypothesis; it is not a logically established theory.[1]

---

[1] See Darwin, "Origin of Species," especially ch. iv. The following statements, from favoring authorities, are weighty and significant:

"Mr. Darwin's remarkable speculation on the Origin of Species is another unimpeachable example of a legitimate hypothesis. What he terms 'natural selection' is not only a *vera causa* [*lex?*], but one proved to be capable of producing effects of the same kind with those which the hypothesis ascribes to it; the question of possibility is entirely one of degree. It is unreasonable to accuse Mr. Darwin (as has been done) of violating the rules of Induction. The rules of Induction are concerned with the conditions of Proof. Mr. Darwin has never

Other examples of approved doctrine wholly hypothetical are Dalton's atomic hypothesis, so prominent in chemistry, and Boscovich's hypothesis of the ultimate mechanical constitution of matter, which holds its place in physics. Such double assumptions of both cause and law must be classed as representative fictions until discovery take them out of this category. Though mere speculations, yet they have scientific value, in promoting unity of conception and suggesting lines of fruitful investigation.

Finally, an hypothesis may be made respecting the law of an effect, the cause and its law being unknown and unsought. Thus Kepler made and rejected, because unverifiable, nineteen hypotheses respecting the orbit of Mars, before he supposed it to be an ellipse,

pretended that his doctrine was proved. He was not bound by the rules of Induction, but by those of Hypothesis. And these last have seldom been more completely fulfilled. He has opened a path of inquiry full of promise, the results of which none can foresee. And is it not a wonderful feat of scientific knowledge and ingenuity to have rendered so bold a suggestion—which the first impulse of every one was to reject at once—admissible and discussible even as a conjecture?"
—Mill, *Logic*, p. 355, note.

"It must suffice to enunciate the belief that Life under all its forms has arisen by a progressive, unbroken evolution; and through the instrumentality of what we call natural causes. That this is an hypothesis, I readily admit. That it may never be anything more, seems probable. That even in its most defensible shape there are serious difficulties in its way, I cheerfully acknowledge. . . . Save for those who still adhere to the Hebrew myth, or to the doctrine of special creations derived from it, there is no alternative but this hypothesis or no hypothesis. For myself, finding that there is *no* positive evidence of special creations, and that there is *some* positive evidence of evolution, I adopt the hypothesis until better instructed."—Herbert Spencer, *Principles of Psychology*, § 208, note (2d ed., 1870).

and found this verifiable (§10). Of like sort is his hypothesis of the law of refraction of light.

§ 86. An hypothesis, whatever approbation it may enjoy, if it be found irreconcilable by any modification with an observed fact—facts being stubborn things—must be abandoned. That heat is a mode of molecular motion was once, but is no longer, an approved doctrine of physics. The system of cycles and epicycles, proposed by Tycho Brahe to account for the celestial motions, fell away as soon as the relative distances of the planets was measured. Frequently, in the history of science, two or more hypotheses, each having its advocates, have been proposed to explain the same class of phenomena. Thus, in electricity, Franklin's hypothesis of one fluid was opposed by Symmes's hypothesis of two fluids; both are now rejected as failing to accord with the facts.

A fact that decides between two rival hypotheses was called by Bacon an *instantia crucis*, a crucial instance.[1] When the Copernican system opposed the Ptolemaic, it triumphed by the *instantia crucis* of aberration of light, a fact incompatible with the earth's being at rest. Foucault's pendulum experiment also is crucial against its immobility. Rival hypotheses of light mark the early history of that science. Newton's emission hypothesis supposes light to

---

[1] It is the fourteenth of his Prerogatives of Instances, introduced thus: "Inter prærogativas instantiarum ponemus, loco decimo quarto, *instantias crucis;* translato vocabulo a crucibus, quæ erectæ in biviis, indicant et signant viarum separationes."—*Nov. Org.*, bk. ii., aph. 36.

consist of minute actual particles emitted with great velocity from luminous bodies. The undulatory hypothesis of Huyghens, already cited (§ 84), supposes light to consist in the vibrations of an elastic luminiferous ether filling space. The absence of mechanical energy from rays of light, the most delicate experiments failing to discover any *vis viva* in the concentrated solar beam, is a negative *instantia crucis* against the emission hypothesis; one positive is that, by this hypothesis, the velocity of light on passing into a denser medium should increase, whereas it was shown by Fizeau to diminish, being in inverse ratio to the refractive indices. Moreover, Fresnel showed that the phenomena of diffraction and of thin plates are inconsistent with this hypothesis, but clearly explicable on the other.[1] These crucial instances overthrew the Newtonian hypothesis, and that of Huyghens has ever since been unrivalled. But let not the disproof of one be mistaken for proof of the other. In general, that an hypothesis has no rival, and is not likely to have one, though it strengthen presumption, is not proof.

§ 87. A special function of verification, then, is to establish a crucial instance which will discredit a rival hypothesis. When this is done, it makes a deep impression, and strengthens the erroneous notion, so common even among scientific thinkers, that verification somehow is proof. We have already stated

[1] See Fresnel's view more fully detailed in Herschel, *Discourse, etc.*, § 218. See, also, Ganot, *Éléments de Physique*, §§ 429, 551.

that its general function is to confirm hypothesis, to heighten its probability (§ 79). When verifications are numerous and unexpected, and conform to the hypothesis with mathematical precision, and especially when defeating all proposed rivals, they almost irresistibly convince. Although any mere hypothesis may at least conceivably be replaced by some other one not yet devised, it is only the strong and clear mind that can successfully resist being misled by such verifications into a confidence proper to empirical certainty alone (§ 45). Mere verifications can never amount to strict proof.[1] Of this much only may we be sure—if the hypothesis of a cause, as the luminiferous ether, be at all tenable, then its laws and the laws of the real cause, whatever it may be, are at least partially identical. But this identity of law does not prove identity of cause, for agencies quite distinct may have identical law; thus the intensity of all radiants—light, heat, gravity, and others—varies inversely as the square of the distance.

The power of predicting entirely new phenomena has been regarded as a specific mark of the truth of an hypothesis.[2] For instance, it being known that

---

[1] An exception, however, should perhaps be taken in case of an hypothesis relative to a single fact, or a group of facts having known limits. Thus, from the hypothesis that the world is round was inferred, it may be circumnavigated; which was first fully verified by the *Vittoria*, one of Magellan's ships, in 1519-21. Cf. the discovery of the planet Neptune, § 11.

[2] So Dr. Whewell seems to think. See *Phil. of Dis.*, ch. xxii., § 51. A very striking case is the prediction, resulting from mathematical deduction, by Sir William R. Hamilton, verified by Dr. Humphrey

two aerial sound waves may so interfere with one another as to produce silence, analogy suggested that, if the undulatory hypothesis of light be true, two rays may so encounter as to neutralize each other, and produce darkness; which prediction was fulfilled on experiment. This, construed as an argument in proof of the hypothesis, is plainly *fallacia consequentis* (§ *145*). A fact thus obtained is only one more added to those already found to accord with the hypothesis. If the law of the propagation of light agrees with that of elastic fluids in a number of known particulars, we may expect it to agree in others. That a fact was predicted does not in the least affect its character or bearing. The fulfilment of such a prophecy merely adds the weight of another verifying fact to a still unproved assumption. Let us remember that Newton formed an hypothesis from which he predicted the combustibility of the diamond; which prediction has proved true, yet the hypothesis has proved false (§ 47).

§ 88. If, then, verification cannot accomplish logical proof, by what process shall it be attained? The form is quite simple.

First, the hypothesis in question must be shown competent to explain all the facts of that class to which it is applied; that is, it must lead deductively to those facts, which deduction is tested by verification.[1]

Ward of Dublin, of the refraction of a single ray of light, under special conditions, into a conical pencil.

[1] The undulatory hypothesis of light fails even here. It gives no

Second, it must be shown that no other hypothesis can explain all the facts; in other words, that any other hypothesis will lead to some false result.[1]

When these two steps have been taken, the proof is complete, passing beyond the highest probability that can be attained by the first step alone, and becoming physical or moral certainty—that is, empirical certainty (§ 45). The thesis is no longer an hypothesis, an unproved proposition, but has become a proved proposition, an established theory.

It is worthy of remark that both parts of this process are often recognized in vulgar speech as requisite to constitute proof. When a supposition is proposed to account for some commonplace affair, and questioned, the proposer is apt to say something like this: *It explains the whole matter, and the thing can't be explained in any other way*, or, *no other explanation will do*. The objector may perhaps reply: *It seems to me some other explanation might be found*, or *is possible*, which also implies that establishing the negative is essential to proof. So in the courts. Circumstantial evidence of guilt, which indeed may be completely refuted by an *alibi*, a fact irreconcilable with the supposition, is accumulated until, in the opinion of both judge and jury, this and no other supposition can possibly explain the facts; which result in ordinary cases will justify

---

satisfactory account of the reflection of light, of the composite character of white light, of the colors of objects, of the absorption of light, or of its chemical and vital influences.

[1] This is essentially the *argumentum ad impossibile* (§ *108*).

condemnation, the indictment becoming morally certain. If the defendant can maintain some other plausible supposition, doubt remains, and he is entitled to the benefit of the doubt—that is, his guilt is not proved.

A little consideration will discover that this process is the rigorous method of difference, the two steps just described fulfilling its condition of affirmative and negative instances (§ 56). For example, it has been observed by Hyene of France, and Bizzolero of Italy, that in every case of the blood of consumptives examined there is present a third corpuscle on which the also ever-present consumption bacillus apparently feeds. The hypothesis is that their coexistence, A, is the cause of the disease, z, which is thereby explained. Allowing that the observed facts support, as above stated, this hypothesis, we have the affirmative instance, $A\ B\ C$ with $y\ z\ x$, the added letters representing other physical circumstances in a case. The numerous confirmatory observations, therefore, by the method of agreement alone, render the hypothetic causal relation highly probable.

Now, the supposition that the third corpuscle alone may be the cause is precluded by the observation that its presence is consistent with health. The supposition that the bacillus alone is the cause remains. Dr. Watkins of New York city resolved to test this last supposition in his own person. Having ascertained that the third corpuscle was not present in his blood, he caused himself to be inoculated with the cultus of tubercule bacilli. The ninety days, during which symptoms of consumption or tuberculosis should appear, passed away without the sign. Thus was supplied the negative instance, $B\ C$ with $x\ y$, required by the method of difference; both the combination of the corpuscle with the bacillus, A, and the disease, z, being absent. Therefore, by this cogent method, the combination is proved to be the cause, no other hypothesis will answer, and the one laid down becomes a fairly established theory, which may lead to very important therapeutic results.

§ 89. The discussion may fitly close with a citation of a standard example. It is Newton's use of the hypothetical form of the deductive method to determine the primary laws of the orbital motion of the planets.[1]

First, he assumed that the force which constantly deflects a planet from a rectilinear course, making it describe a curve around the sun, tends directly toward the sun. Then he proved deductively that, if it do so, the radius vector of its orbit shall describe equal areas in equal times. This was verified by being identical with Kepler's first law, already empirically ascertained (§ 10 n.). Newton then proved that if the force acted in any other direction whatever, the radius vector would not describe equal areas in equal times, which consequent is false to fact. This latter step completes the proof of the first assumption.

---

[1] In the following statement we follow pretty closely the excellent analysis of Mr. Mill, *Logic*, p. 351.

For, let A be a force acting centrally; $A\ B\ C$, the planets and a central force; $B\ C$, the planets apart from a central force. Now the planets and a central force produce z, areas proportional to the times, with $x\ y$, effects other than z; the planets apart from a central force produce $x\ y$ only. Hence it is rigorously proved by the method of difference that A, a force acting centrally, is the causal law of z, areas as the times.

Second, having thus determined the direction of the deflecting force, Newton proceeded in like manner to ascertain the law of quantitative variation of that force. He assumed that the force varies inversely as the square of the distance. From this he deduced Kepler's second and third laws, which verified the hypothesis. He then proved that any other law of variation would give results inconsistent with Kepler's laws already known to be true. This completes the proof of the second assumption.

Newton then used these conclusions as premises under which, by the direct deductive method, the motion of the moon was brought as a special or particular case, and terrestrial gravity proved to be its cause. This argument is detailed in § 79.

Thus was established the theory of universal gravitation. The general induction which immediately follows the foregoing specific proofs is stated by Newton as an obvious and necessary inference. He says: "If it universally appears, by experiments and astronomical observations, that all bodies about the earth gravitate towards the earth, and that in proportion to the quantity of matter which they severally contain; that the moon likewise, according to the quantity of its matter, gravitates towards the earth; that, on the other hand, our sea gravitates towards the moon; and all the planets mutually one towards another; and the comets in like manner towards the sun; we must universally allow that all bodies whatsoever are endowed with a principle of mutual gravitation."[1] Subsequently he says: "We have explained the phenomena of the heavens by the power of gravity, but have not assigned the cause of this power. Hitherto I have not been able to discover the cause of the properties of gravity from phenomena, and apart from phenomena I frame no hypotheses. It is enough that gravity does really exist, and act according to the laws which we have explained, and abundantly serves to account for all the motions of celestial bodies."[2]

[1] *Principia*, bk. iii., under Rule 3d.   [2] Id., *Scholium Generale*.

XII.—NATURAL LAW

§ 90. The ultimate essence in the generic notion law is similarity. When a number of facts, either beings or events, make a striking impression of similarity, each is regarded as a repetition of the others. A phenomenon is said to be repeated when the mind of the observer receives impressions so very similar as to be indistinguishable except as to time or place. When several such impressions concur, the notion of repetition is expanded into the notion of order. This, when the order is undeviating, becomes the notion of strict uniformity. Law expresses strict uniformity. Its most general definition may be stated thus:

A law is a designation of a constant order of facts determined by the constitution of the things.[1]

---

[1] The synthesis of this section is of elements obtained by an analysis of the notion law. A *designation* simply marks out and makes known. The *things* are those from which the law arises, and to which it applies. The *constitution* is an assemblage of properties, which properties, being constant causes, *determine* both the *facts* and their *constant order*. The specific difference, *determined*, etc., excludes voluntary order (*e. g.* that discovered by statistics of crime), chance order (§ 49), and any order discernible in primitive collocations (§ 94 n.).

§ 91. Primarily there are two kinds of law—formal law and material law.

Formal laws designate or give expression to the forms in which the mind conceives of things. They are strictly abstract formulas, occasioned by the order of phenomena, but expressing only the consequent intellectual order necessary to the understanding of phenomena. Such are the primary laws of logic, the principles of induction, the axioms of mathematics, the fundamental principle of ethics, and any other primary axiomatic truth of pure intuition (§ 7). A formal law arising from demonstration—that is, one deduced *a priori* from axioms—is a secondary formal law; as, the dicta of the syllogism, the canons of causation, the law of a mathematical series, and the like. Formal laws are expressive of ultimate abstract absolute truth.

Material laws designate formal or conceptional order incorporated with matter, and thereby give expression to phenomenal order. The order of phenomena is always determined by the constitution of the things themselves, which order is recognized by the observer, and formulated as material law.

The term has in good usage such wide and varied applications that it is difficult to formulate an accurate and adequate definition.

Montesquieu defines thus: "Laws in their most extended signification are the necessary relations arising from the nature of things." He adds: "In this sense all beings have their laws, the Deity has His laws, the material world has its laws, superior intelligences have their laws, the brutes have their laws, and man has his laws."—*L'Esprit des Lois*, bk. i., ch. 1. This is altogether the most meritorious attempt I have seen to construct a comprehensive definition of law.

§ 92. Material law likewise is of two kinds, moral law and natural law.

Moral law, apart from its content, has the form of a categorical imperative: *Act by a maxim fitly universal.* This materialized becomes: *Trespass not; Love thy neighbor.* It is a mandate addressed to persons, implying a possible alternative, and the required order, determined by the natural constitution of its subjects, is sanctioned by authority, power, and penalty. The decalogue, all civil, common, and statute law, and even the conventions of polite society, are specialized statements of moral law.

Natural law generalizes and formulates facts of coexistence and events of orderly succession in inanimate things, and also in animate beings apart from their free will. It merely states a uniformity which has been found to exist in nature.

Moral law is in form imperative; natural law is simply indicative. The one is a uniformity enjoined, having an alternative; the other is a uniformity established, having no alternative. In the one the facts come after the law; in the other the facts come before the law. The one generalizes ideal facts that ought to be; the other, real facts that actually are. Moral law of actions becomes known *a priori* by pure intuition, and serves as a premise from which to deduce specific rules of duty in personal conduct; natural laws of events become known *a posteriori* by induction, and serve as premises from which to deduce specific laws and particular facts of science, and rules of art.

In addition to these distinctions let us clear the notions of two adhering misconceptions.

It is probable that the notion law is derived originally from the expressed will of a superior in power and authority.[1] But this meaning has become specific by extending the content of the notion to include generically various uniformities, though still retaining, in perhaps all of its applications, a covert suggestion of authoritative imposition. Hence, it may be, arises the confused and inaccurate, yet very common, thinking and speaking of obedience to or violation of natural law. Persons, to whom moral law is addressed, may obey or break it; the alternative is possible. But neither persons nor things literally obey natural law; for, there being no possible alternative, it cannot be violated, or perverted. A planet does not obey the laws of motion and gravitation; the notion of obedience is inapplicable to it. A natural law does not convey a command, it is never expressed in the imperative mood, but is a categorical proposition indicative merely of a general fact in general terms.[2]

---

[1] The word *law* is cognate with *lay*, from the Anglo-Saxon *legu*, and this from the causative *leegan*, to lay down. A law is that which is laid, set, fixed; Lat. *statuere*, whence *statute*. Austin limits it thus: "A law, in the literal and proper sense of the word, may be defined as a rule laid down for the guidance of an intelligent being by an intelligent being having power over him."—*Jurisprudence*, § 2. Again he says: "Every law or rule (taken with the largest signification which can be given to the term properly) is a command."—*Id.*, § 19.

[2] Bishop Hooker in *Ecclesiastical Polity*, after his famous saying of Law, that "her seat is the bosom of God, and her voice is the har-

NATURAL LAW 181

By another very common confusion of thought, laws of both kinds are often spoken of as though they were themselves efficient agents. We hear of the restraint of civil law, and of its compulsive power. As mere metonymy this may be allowed; but with many who speak thus, it is not figurative, but literal. Hence it needs to be pointed out that, while the police and the jailor exert force and are causes, the law which they execute does nothing beyond serving as a mandatory guide. Laws do not govern or regulate men; men regulate themselves, or a governor rules them, according to law.[1] So, likewise, natural laws are often confused with causes. They relate to energy, force, cause, but are in themselves impotent. It is true of causes, but not of laws, that they counteract or interfere with one another, and can

---

mony of the world," complains that men are less subservient to the divine order than are things. Montesquieu, in " L'Esprit des Lois," declaims on the stricter obedience, throughout the universe, of material things to the laws of nature than of mankind to the divine and human laws laid down for their conduct.

"The confusion of Law, in the judicial sense, with Law as a uniformity of nature," says Mr. Bain, "is exemplified in Butler's chapter on the Moral Government of God [*Analogy*, etc., pt. i., ch. 3]. Butler calls the 'course of Nature' a government merely on the ground that it induces precautions to avoid pain. But these precautions have nothing moral in them; they may be used for criminal ends. Guy Fawkes most faithfully obeyed [?] the laws of nature when he placed his barrels of gunpowder so as to insure the blowing up of Parliament, while he arranged for firing them in safety to himself."
—*Logic*, bk. vi., ch. 4.

[1] We note, however, that enacted law inclines law-abiding subjects to observance; also that, as merely contemplated, it is an efficient educator.

be adjusted to an end. As a planet does not obey law, so it is not governed by law, nor even according to law as men are. Nature, amidst its apparently unsettled vacillating diversities, is characterized by certain established unvarying uniformities, which natural laws merely record.[1]

§ 93. Natural law is the product of observation. It indicatively affirms an order of natural facts to be universal—that is, to occur with invariable uniformity. Natural laws are of two kinds: primary or ultimate, and secondary or derivative. The latter kind is subdivided into rational and empirical.[2] The

---

[1] Mr. Mill says: "In minds not habituated to accurate thinking, there is often a confused notion that the general laws are the *causes* of the partial ones; that the law of general gravitation, for example, causes the phenomenon of the fall of bodies to the earth. But to assert this would be a misuse of the word cause; terrestrial gravity is not an effect of general gravitation, but a *case* of it; that is, one kind of the particular instances in which that general law obtains."—*Logic*, p. 338. Notwithstanding this excellent statement, he uses the term *law* in the sense of *cause* many hundred times.

The Duke of Argyll says: "Every Law of Nature is liable to counteraction; and the rule is that laws are habitually made to counteract each other."—*Reign of Law*, ch. ii. (p. 100, Am. ed.). In many places he confuses force with law; e.g., "Force ascertained according to some measure of its operation, is one of the definitions of a scientific Law."—*Id.*, p. 71. Again: "No one Law—that is to say, no one Force—determines anything."—*Id.*, p. 76.

[2] The secondary or derivative laws are the *axiomata media* of Bacon. The terms rational and empirical, marking the subdivision, are not clearly distinctive, are not in proper opposition; but good usage sanctions this specific application of them, and we have none better at hand.

empirical are those of succession and those of coexistence (§ 33). We shall discuss these several kinds in reverse order, the order of inductive generalization.

§ 94. A uniformity of coexistence, an order of facts observed to be simultaneous, to be associated in all cases in wide observation without exception, is recognized as empirical law. Such is the uniform coexistence of inertia and gravity in all bodies. These two properties seem to be entirely independent of each other, and yet are conjoined through all nature, and are proportional in amount. Likewise, body and mind coexist in all men.

In natural kinds are found many coinhering attributes which are cases of uniform coexistence, and so reducible to law; as, *All animals have a nervous superadded to a digestive system.* The group of coexisting attributes marking a natural kind constitutes the law of that kind as expressed in its complete definition. Each being essential, if any one be absent, we have a different kind. Thus a specific weight of 19.3 is essential to gold; if a metal were found having all the other marks of gold with a different specific weight, it would not be gold; it would be a new kind, with a different law.

Sometimes an accidental mark is so persistent as to furnish a quasi-law. Colors, for example, are often quite constant, as that of melted or polished gold and silver, of oak and pine leaves, of crows, and even of men. Negroes are black, Indians are red.

Such coexistences in many cases are properties, and sharply characteristic, as risibility in man (§ *15*). Hence they may serve in a quasi-definition; as, *A dog is a digitigrade quadruped, having fixed claws, four toes, and a recurved tail.* But such generalities, however true, can rarely claim the dignity of law.

The only method applicable to ascertain a law of coexistence is enumeration (§ 37 sq.). Hence such laws are attended by all the hazard and imperfection belonging to that method, and their statements, including definitions of kinds, often undergo modifications from wider experience.[1]

---

[1] There is in nature a large class of coexistences, commonly spoken of as primeval or primordial facts or original agents, which are regarded as ultimate, and beyond explanation or reduction to law. The sun, as to its existence, size, gravitating force, etc., the earth, the planets, with their various constituents of air, water, rocks, and other distinguishable substances, simple and compound, both as to quantity and quality, of which these various bodies are made up, are primordial facts. The nebular hypothesis of Kant and Laplace seeks to go beyond their known *status*, and to explain broadly their origin. But so long as we can give no satisfactory account of their origin, of their distribution in space, of their relative quantities, they are provisionally classed as primeval coexisting natural agents. Their distribution and relative quantities are so irregular as to seem casual and lawless. They are mere collocations, and mere collocations cannot be reduced to any law. Hence, what we know of them furnishes no ground for an induction respecting the distribution and quantities of similar bodies in remoter space. They are permanent causes in nature as it is, but are themselves without assignable cause. As the truths of pure reason are the ultimate basis of the laws of thought, so in a sense are these permanent causes the ultimate basis of the laws of things; in the one case we cannot assign a *reason*, in the other, a *cause*.

§ 95. An empirical law in general is a secondary or derivative law, the derivation of which is not yet known. It is an ascertained uniformity attributed to causation, and hence presumed to be resolvable into simpler laws, but not yet resolved. It is not original, and remains to be accounted for.

Empirical laws are inductions by the methods of enumeration or agreement, by which methods alone causation cannot be proved. Indeed, almost all truths obtained by simple observation, including laws of coexistence, are to be regarded as empirical, and the hazard that attends them is such that scientists hesitate to rely upon them in cases varying much from those actually observed.

Laws of succession yet empirical are: The local laws of tides; Red sunset betokens fair weather; Breeds are improved by crossing; Boiling temperature destroys animal life; An alloy is harder than its components; The number of atoms of acid neutralizing an atom of base is equal to the number of atoms of oxygen in the base. Harvey's law, *Omne vivum ex ovo*, is empirical. So also is the law of continuity, *Natura non agit per saltum*, which is illustrated in the continuity of animal and vegetable life, and in general by the transition of matter from one state into another, as in melting, boiling, and their opposites. The attempt to fill apparent gaps in nature's continuity stated in this law has led to important discoveries, having the character of verifications (§ 87), but the law is unproved, unexplained, and so empirical. True, the development hypothesis offers a partial explanation, which, however, is merely hypothetical (§ 85).[1]

The medical sciences furnish good illustrations. Anatomy is strictly empirical, since it is concerned wholly with the manner of the distribution of the various parts of the organism. Physiology, which is concerned with the functions of these parts, has made some progress towards rational explanation, but, owing to the vast complexity of the subject, its advance is slow and hesitating. Pathology only quite recently has given promise of passing successfully, through hypothesis, from the empirical to the rational stage. The old humoral hypothesis of Galen, and the solidist hypothesis of Hoffman and Cullen, were long rivals as explanations of disease (§ 86). Both are now superseded by the germ hypothesis, which bids fair to become established theory (§ 88). Infectious diseases are attributed to bacteria. The specific bacillus of tuberculosis, of

---

[1] The following Laws of the Reflection of Light are empirical:

I. The angle of reflection is equal to the angle of incidence.

II. The incident and the reflected ray are both in the same plane, which is perpendicular to the reflecting surface.

Also Descartes' Laws of Single Refraction, as follow:

I. Whatever the obliquity of the incident ray, the ratio which the sine of the incident angle bears to the sine of the angle of refraction is constant for the same two media, but varies with different media.

II. The incident and the refracted ray are in the same plane which is perpendicular to the surface separating the two media.—Ganot, *Éléments de Physique*, §§ 440, 461.

These Laws of Refraction have received a fitting explanation on the undulatory hypothesis, but it is merely hypothetical (§ 84).

cholera, of diphtheria, of typhoid fever, and others, have been isolated, and numerous experiments tried, with the result that no one now thinks of humor or of disorganized tissue as the cause of disease, but that such or such a bacillus has invaded the body, and caused a specific disorder. Therapeutics lingers in the rear. There is some rational hygienic or constitutional treatment, but the use of drugs is almost exclusively empirical— their *modus operandi* can rarely be explained. That quinine checks fever, that table-salt checks hemorrhage, are empirical facts inductively generalized. They are doubtless derivative from some higher uniformities, but as yet are unexplained. Indeed, therapeutics is so largely empirical that it can hardly be deemed scientific, but is rather an art having a body of narrow and precarious rules to guide the practitioner, rules for which no aprioric reason can be assigned, and of which it can only be said that their observance has been remedial in similar cases. Hence the hesitation of wise physicians, their careful, tentative, watchful procedure with each new patient.

§ 96. By the term rational law in this connection is meant merely law that can be deductively derived from more general laws, or, in other words, that can be resolved into primary laws. The derived law is thereby rationally explained.

Thus the distribution of land and water, the stratification of the earth's crust, the occurrence of heavy metals in deep mines, of corrosible metals in combination, of the non-corrosible, as gold and platinum, in a pure state—all are cases of evident causation, and are referable to more general laws.

In the progress of knowledge it not infrequently happens, as already intimated, that what was once merely an empirical law is resolved into well-ascertained uniformities of wider scope, and thus becomes a rational law. The presence of snow on high mountains was at one time only an empirical uniformity, but we now resolve it into the laws of radiant heat, and of condensation and freezing of vapor. Previous to the discovery of the pressure of the atmosphere, the rise of water under the action of a pump, and the standing height of mercury in the Torricellian tube, were known only as narrow empirical generalties. Now they are conjointly explained by reference to their common cause—atmospheric pressure—acting in accord with Pascal's more general law of pressure, which law, in turn, is deducible from the still more general laws of fluidity and gravity.[1]

---

[1] The following is Pascal's Law of Liquid Pressure:

Pressure exerted anywhere upon a mass of liquid is transmitted undiminished in all directions, and acts with the same force on all equal surfaces, and in a direction at right angles to those surfaces.

Also the Laws of the Equilibrium of Floating Bodies are neat examples of rational derivative laws, as follow:

I. The floating body must displace a volume of liquid whose weight equals that of the body.

II. The centre of gravity of the floating body must be in the same vertical line with that of the fluid displaced.

III. The equilibrium of a floating body is stable or unstable according as the metacentre is above or below the centre of gravity.—Ganot, *Eléments de Physique*, §§ 89, 106.

The periodical return of eclipses, as known to the Chaldean astrologers, was an empirical law, until the general laws of the celestial motions accounted for it. Kepler's laws, as established by him, were merely empirical generalizations (§ 10 n.). They ceased so to be, and became rational derivative laws when Newton deduced them from the three laws of motion (§ 89).

Rational derivative laws are very often conditioned for realization upon specific collocations of primeval agents (§ 94 n.). The uniformity, though invariable while the agents coexist, would cease to be should that coexistence cease.[1] The orderly succession of day and night, the round of the seasons, the ebb and flow of the sea, are dependent on the earth's diurnal rotation, the inclination of its equator to the ecliptic, and the relative position of earth, sun, and moon. So long as these collocations, of which no account can be given, are maintained, the uniformities result, and are rationally derivative, from the laws of motion and of gravity. We can calculate on finding such sequences only where we know by direct evidence that the agents on which they depend are present and fulfil the requisite conditions. The

---

[1] "Derivative laws do not depend solely on the ultimate laws into which they are resolvable; they mostly depend on those ultimate laws, and an ultimate fact; namely, the mode of coexistence of some of the component elements of the universe [§ 94, note]. The ultimate laws of causation might be the same as at present, and yet the derivative laws completely different, if the causes coexisted in different proportions, or with any difference in those of their relations by which the effects are influenced."—Mill, *Logic*, p. 367.

law that coal lies above red sandstone holds throughout the earth, but cannot be applied to other planets. The quantity and distribution of water on our globe cannot be assigned to any other; but the proportion of oxygen and hydrogen in water is referable to the ascertained universal laws of affinity or chemical combination, and hence may be safely affirmed wherever in the universe they unite. The coexistence in a definite proportion of oxygen and nitrogen in our atmosphere cannot be predicated of any other atmosphere; but their uniform intermixture, wherever they occur, may be predicated, for the law of the diffusion of gases is a universal natural law.)

§ 97. Something needs to be said in this connection about explanation. First, let us ask what is meant by a mystery, a marvel, a curiosity, an unaccountable fact, a strange event, an extraordinary phenomenon. It means simply an isolated fact, one not standing in any known order of things, not referable to a class, or a cause, or a law, and hence exciting curiosity and wonder; as the zodiacal light, the aurora borealis. Likewise a comet is not referable, perhaps, to any narrower class than cosmical body, which reference is so far from being satisfactory that we still say it is a curious thing. Why is its coma always turned from the sun? The fact is strange, wonderful, unaccountable. Familiarity with an isolated fact will abate emotion, still an explanation is always acceptable.[1]

[1] "It is a common illusion to regard phenomena as simple because

A fact, then, either particular or general, is said to be explained when it is assigned to a well-known class of things, or when its cause is ascertained, or when the law or laws of causation, of which it is an instance, are indicated. I pick up a brilliant stone, and am told it is a crystal of quartz; a fire destroys a dwelling, because a lamp was overturned; a balloon ascends, for the surrounding air, being heavier, pushes it upward, in accord with the law of gravitating fluids. These facts are thus explained, at least partially. So also a law or uniformity of nature is said to be explained when another law or laws are pointed out of which the law in question is a case, and from which it could be deduced, into which it could be resolved. An explanation very often is provisionally merely hypothetical, reducible perhaps to theory by subsequent proof, but commonly we have to be content with a plausible supposition (§§ 78, 79). Explanation, then, in a philosophical sense, is the reference of a fact to its class, cause, or law; or else the resolution of an empirical uniformity into laws of causation, real or hypothetical, from which it logically results, or the resolving a complex law of

they are familiar. Very familiar facts seem to stand in no need of explanation themselves, and to be the means of explaining whatever can be assimilated to them. Thus the boiling and evaporation of a liquid is supposed to be a very simple phenomenon requiring no explanation, and a satisfactory medium of the explanation of rarer phenomena. That water should dry up is, to the uninstructed mind, a thing wholly intelligible; whereas, to the man acquainted with physical science, the liquid state is anomalous and inexplicable."— Bain, *Logic*, bk. iii., ch. 12, § 10.

causation into simpler and more general ones from which it is capable of being deductively inferred.[1]

Let it be remarked that, after all, explanation is merely substituting one mystery for another. It does nothing to render the general course of nature other than mysterious; for the highest ambition of natural science and its loftiest reach is to attain to primordial agents, and to such ultimate laws as are incapable of physical explanation, and only more mysterious because of their wider comprehension. Natural theology with teleology, assuming the supernatural, carries the explanation still further, but

---

[1] In loose and general expression, to account for or explain anything is to connect it with known things. The connection, real or hypothetical, is either by similarity or by causation. We bring other things to stand under it, and so it becomes understood by means of them. The quasi-definition *a posteriori* (§ 38) in most of its forms is merely an explanation. Says Lotze: "To explain means nothing more than to show that a definite event is the result of its antecedents in accordance with general rules."—*Grundzüge der Praktischen Philosophie*, § 20.

"Scientific explanation and inductive generalization, being the same thing, the limits of explanation are the limits of induction. The limits to inductive generalization are the limits to the agreement or community of facts. . . . Newton seemed unable to acquiesce in gravity as an ultimate fact. It was inconceivable to him that matter should act upon other matter at a distance, and he therefore desired a medium of operation, whereby gravity might be assimilated to impact. But this assimilation has hitherto been impracticable; if so, gravity is an ultimate fact, and its own sufficing and final explanation. The acceptance of this is the proper scientific attitude of mind. . . . We are utterly ignorant how matter and mind operate on each other. Properly speaking, there is nothing to be known but the fact, generalized to the utmost."—Bain, *Logic*, bk. iii., ch. 12, §§ 6, 11. See "Psychology," § 122, note.

with like termination in the great mystery of mysteries.[1]

§ 98. Passing now to the class of natural laws marked as primary or ultimate, we observe that these are called, *par excellence,* Laws of Nature, a title that in usage is denied to the secondary or derivative laws. How shall they be described so as to distinguish them within the comprehending class of natural laws? First, they are free from the condition, to which so many derivative laws are subjected, of a special collocation of primeval agents (§ 96). Secondly, they are the fewest and simplest

---

[1] Dr. Whewell, in *Nov. Org. Renov.,* bk. iii., ch. 10, § 7, says, very beautifully, of the Supreme Cause: "In the utterance of Science, no cadence is heard with which the human mind can feel satisfied. Yet we cannot but go on listening for and expecting a satisfactory close. The notion of a cadence appears to be essential to our relish of the music. The idea of some closing strain seems to lurk among our own thoughts, waiting to be articulated in the notes which flow from the knowledge of external nature. The idea of something ultimate in our philosophical researches, something in which the mind can acquiesce, and which will leave us no further questions to ask, of *whence* and *why,* and *by what power,* seems as if it belonged to us, as if we could not have it withheld from us by any imperfection or incompleteness in the actual performances of science. What is the meaning of this conviction? What is the reality thus anticipated? Whither does the development of this Idea conduct us?

"We have already seen that a difficulty of the same kind, which arises in the contemplation of causes and effects considered as forming an historical series, drives us to the assumption of a First Cause, as an axiom to which our idea of causation in time necessarily leads. And as we were thus guided to a First Cause in order of Succession, the same kind of necessity directs us to a Supreme Cause in order of Causation."

general truths from which the multifarious uniformities in nature may be deductively inferred, or those widest inductions which, being granted, will account for the existing order of nature. Accordingly, they are reckoned as primary or ultimate—that is, original and underived. But let us not be misled by these expressions to understand that science claims to have reached this high ideal. Since we are continually discovering that uniformities, previously considered ultimate, are derivative, resolvable into more general laws, we cannot be sure that any of the recognized laws of nature are strictly ultimate, though well assured that there must be ultimate laws, and that every such resolution brings us nearer to them. Thus the laws of magnetic agency having been affiliated with the laws of electric action, both have ever since been considered as special cases referable to more general laws of electricity.

The three Laws of Motion (§ 18 n.) may be cited as notable examples of laws of nature, their great simplicity and wide comprehension rendering a further reduction hardly possible. This high rank is sustained by a special characteristic which is worthy of remark. Whatever may have been the actual logical process by which their discoverer evolved them (§ 72), now that we have them they are seen to be true *a priori*. As soon as their terms are clearly understood, they are accepted as necessarily and universally true. They approach very nearly the character of formal laws (§ 91). Although not entirely pure, not wholly free from empirical matter, yet they are so highly abstract that they deal rather with mathematical ideas than with mechanical facts. Like the simpler theorems of geometry, they are so directly deducible from pure axioms, combined with the simple empirical facts of motion, change, and force, that even *a priori* proof is needless, and they are posited as the axioms of mechanics. Though not strictly self-evident, they are evidently and absolutely true, which means, not merely that no exception is possible, but also that no exception is conceivable. This puts them above the plane of inductive truth, whose highest reach is empirical certainty.[1]

The most illustrious example of a law of nature is the Law of Universal Gravitation, the culmination of Newton's research (§§ 79, 89). Its statement is: Every body of matter in the universe tends towards every other with a force that is directly as its mass, and inversely as the square of the distance. Consider for a moment the great number and variety of special uniformities, both particular cases and consequences, which are accounted for by this very simple and universal law of nature. The single fact of a tendency of every particle towards every other, varying inversely as the distance squared, explains the fall of bodies to the ground, the revolutions of

---

[1] See §§ 7, 45. Newton's own title for these laws is *Axiomata sive Leges Motûs*. The laws of motion and the moral law (§ 92) are strikingly similar in respect of this characteristic—that both may be inductively evolved, and both are intuitively true.

the planets and their satellites, the motion of comets, and all the various regularities that have been observed in these special phenomena, such as the elliptical orbits, and the variations from exact ellipses known as perturbations, the relation between the solar distances of the planets and the periodic times of their revolutions, the precession of the equinoxes, the tidal motions, and a vast number of minor astronomical and terrestrial truths.

The discovery of the universal Laws of Energy marks an important epoch in modern science.[1] It accomplished not only a unification of many branches of physics previously regarded as distinct, but also

---

[1] See § 17. The following are the Laws of Energy:

I. TRANSFER OF ENERGY.—Energy may be transferred from one body to another, but only by work done between them and to the extent of the work done.

II. TRANSFORMATION OF ENERGY.—Energy may be transformed (with or without transfer) from kinetic to potential or from potential to kinetic, or from some variety of one to a different variety of either, but only by work and to the extent of the work done.

III. DEGRADATION OF ENERGY.—The quantity of energy that in any operation takes the form of heat, is said to be dissipated. This law is often called the law of dissipation of energy.

IV. CONSERVATION OF ENERGY.—In any system or collection of bodies, the sum total of energy is not altered by the transfers and transformations taking place between the members of the system themselves. That sum total can be altered only by exchanges between these members and other bodies not belonging to the system. Energy is not altered in amount by transfer or transformation. The mutual actions of natural bodies neither create nor destroy energy. What one body gains, some other body loses.

This statement of the Laws of Energy is taken from *Outlines of Physics* (part ii., §§ 21, 23, 30, 31), by Professor F. H. Smith, LL.D., of the University of Virginia.

has explained for the first time a multitude of special phenomena in each branch, and by prediction has led to lines of new research resulting in many brilliant discoveries.

The Laws of Chemical Combination, from which the whole science of chemistry is derived, are very simple and very wide generalizations, which, being regarded provisionally as ultimate, rank as laws of nature.[1]

§ 99. The great object of the scientist is to obtain by rigid induction the laws of nature, and to follow them by rigid deduction to their consequences. A science at first wholly inductive becomes, as soon as a law has been proved, more or less deductive, and as it progresses, rising to higher and wider but fewer inductions, the deductive processes increase in number and importance, until it is no longer properly

---

[1] The Laws of Chemical Combination are as follow:

I. DEFINITE PROPORTIONS.—In every chemical compound the nature and the proportions of its constituent elements are fixed, definite, and invariable.

II. MULTIPLE PROPORTIONS.—If two elements, A and B, unite together in more proportions than one, on comparing together quantities of the different compounds, each of which contains the same amount of A, the quantities of B will bear a very simple relation to each other.

III. EQUIVALENT PROPORTIONS.—Each elementary substance, in combining with other elements, or in displacing others from their combinations, does so in a fixed proportion, which may be represented numerically.

These laws are taken from Miller's *Elements of Chemistry*, part i., Chemical Physics, §§ 9, 10, 11.

an inductive, but a deductive science. Thus hydrostatics, acoustics, optics, and electricity, commonly called inductive sciences, have passed under the dominion of mathematics, and mechanics in general has a like history (§ 73). Celestial mechanics as founded in the "Principia" of Newton is mainly inductive, as elaborated in the "Mécanique Céleste" of Laplace is mainly deductive. By pursuing this latter process it has multiplied its matter, and reached its present high perfection. A revolution is quietly progressing in all the natural sciences. Bacon changed their method from deductive to inductive, and it is now rapidly reverting from inductive to deductive. The task of logic is to explicate and regulate these methods.[1]

[1] Bacon, in *Distributio Operis*, 6th paragraph, and in *Nov. Org.*, bk. i., aph. 11 sq., speaks disparagingly of the syllogism. The chief aim of his *Instauratio* is to forbid the *saltus*, usual in previous science, from a simple enumeration of particulars at once to the widest generalities, and to require a graduated procedure. In aph. 19, he says: "There are and can be but two ways of investigating and discovering truth. The one hurries on rapidly from the senses and particulars to the most general laws; and from them as principles and their supposed indisputable truth derives and discovers the intermediate laws [*axiomata media*]. The other constructs its laws from the senses and particulars by ascending continuously and gradually till it finally arrives at the most general laws, which is the true but unattempted way." In aph. 22, he adds: "Each of these two ways begins from the senses and particulars, and ends in the greatest generalities. But they are immensely different; for the one merely touches cursorily on particulars and experiment, whilst the other runs duly and regularly through them; the one, from the very outset, lays down some abstract and useless generalities, the other gradually rises to such as are naturally better fitted to be the object of knowledge." Cf. aph. 104, and see the quotation in our § 40, note.

§ 100. Unity, says Plato, is the end of philosophy. It is a fair question whether the laws of nature may not, in the advance of knowledge, be resolved into some one all-comprehensive law, thus attaining the philosophical ideal. In considering this, let it be observed that all scientific investigation of natural facts and laws is in order to obtain a philosophical explanation of phenomena. Now, a phenomenon is that which appears to an observer (§ 33). The word, therefore, is a relative term, the name of a relation between a natural fact and a percipient intelligence. It follows that phenomena may be ultimately reducible to as many kinds as there are kinds of sense-perception, but that they cannot be reduced to any fewer kinds than the number of sense-perceptions that are distinct or irreducible to one another. Therefore, the ultimate laws of nature are necessarily as

---

The limitations of human knowledge and power are indicated in aphorisms 1-10. These the closing passage of *Dist. Op.* anticipates, saying: "Man, the minister and interpreter of nature, does and understands as much as he has observed of the order, operation, and mind of nature, and neither knows nor is able to do more. Neither is it possible for any power to loosen or burst the chain of causes, nor is nature to be overcome except by submission. Therefore these two objects, human knowledge and power, are really the same; and failure in action chiefly arises from the ignorance of causes. For everything depends on our fixing the mind's eye steadily in order to receive their images exactly as they exist, and may God never permit us to give out the dream of our fancy as a model of the world, but rather in his kindness vouchsafe to us the means of writing a revelation and true vision of the traces and stamps of the Creator on his creatures." Then follows a Prayer which the present writer humbly makes his own.

many at least as the distinct kinds of perception, and can never be reduced to one comprehensive law.

In illustration of this we note that the perception of color is radically distinct from the perception of sound. True, they are strikingly similar in several respects, especially in their causes, both being produced by molecular vibration. But this reduction is only apparent, for these causes, as well as their laws, are themselves irreducibly distinct. Hence there must always be a law connecting molecular motion with color, and another law connecting molecular motion with sound. Moreover, color and sound are effects intrinsically and essentially unlike, and since unlike effects have unlike causes (§ 23), these phenomena can never be referred to causes strictly alike, or to a common cause or law. Heat, light, and electricity are convertible forms of energy, but essentially distinct in their laws, because their several phenomena are presented to distinct modes of perception. The great generalizations of force producing molar motion, as the laws of motion and gravity, are all referable ultimately to muscular sense-perception, which stands distinctly and irreducibly apart from the phenomena of the other senses. Thus it is that the ultimate laws of nature cannot be less numerous than the ultimate powers of perception.

INDEX

(*The number refers to the page.*)

Accidents, induction only of, 9.
Agent and patient, 25 n.
Agreement, canon of, 117.
— imperfections of, 122.
— yields probability, 124.
— double method of, 125.
Analogy defined, 62, 69.
— canon of, 69.
— justification of, 71.
— scientific value of, 73.
Analysis of the notion law, 177.
Analytic forms distinguished, 8.
Antecedents and consequents, 24.
— distribution of, 57 n., 121.
Approximate generalization, 81, 96.
Argyll on law of nature, 182 n.
Aristotle's view of induction, 6 n.
— four causes, 23 n.
— formula of induction, 44.
— view of analogy, 68.
— of induction *vs.* deduction, 142.
Axiom of change, 29.
— of uniformity, first, 31.
— of uniformity, second, 35.
— of sufficient reason, 85.
Axioms, their origin, 30.
— Mill's view criticised, 31 n., 67 n.

Bacon on induction, 6 n.
— on enumeration, 62, 67 n.
— on elimination, 104 n.
— his Organon, 142 n., 198 n.
— on crucial instances, 168 n.
— *axiomata media*, 182 n., 198 n.
— on modes of research, 198 n.
— knowledge and power, 199 n.

Bain, definition of induction, 7 n.
— on Butler's view, 181 n.
— on familiarity, 190 n.
— on explanation, 192 n.
Butler, analogical argument, 74.
— on probability, 78.
— criticised by Bain, 181 n.

Canon of enumeration of cases, 63.
— of analogy, 69.
— of probability, 89.
— of perfect induction, 103.
— of difference, 106.
— of residue, 113.
— of agreement, 117.
— of double agreement, 126.
— of concomitant variations, 131.
— of deduction, direct, 150.
Causation, definition of, 28.
— intuitional view of, 30.
— empirical view of, 31 n.
— canons of, 103, 105 n.
Cause, investigation of, 19.
— its general meaning, 22.
— various kinds of, 23 n.
— definition of, 27.
— preventive, 25, 81, 109 n.
— *vs.* law, 181.
— the Supreme, Whewell on, 193 n.
Causes, plurality of, maxim, 37.
Certainty, strict, 76.
— empirical, 77, 83 n.
Chance, its meanings, 29, 82.
— defined; the problem of, 84.
— Laplace's rule, 86.
— first rule of, 86.

Chance, second rule of, 87.
— canon for distinguishing, 89.
Coexistence, phenomena of, 54.
— laws of, 183.
— of collocations, 184 n., 189.
Colligation, 16, 17.
Collocations, 184 n., 189.
Composition of causes, 147, 149.
Comte on use of hypothesis, 162 n.
Concomitant variations, 130.
— canon of, 131.
— illustrations of, 132.
— quantitative value, 135, 137.
Condition, causal, 24, 121.
Crucial instances, 168.

Darwin's hypothesis, 166.
Deduction distinguished, 5.
— its relation to induction, 141.
— authorities quoted on, 142 n.
— related to discovery, 144.
— direct method of, 150.
— canon of, 150.
— three stages of, 151.
— Newton's use of, 153.
— indirect method of, 160.
— three stages of, 161.
— conditions of proof, 171.
— Newton's use of, 174.
Definition of logic, 1.
— of inference, 4.
— of induction, 6, 7 n.
— of cause and of effect, 27.
— of causation, 28.
— of phenomenon, 54.
— of observation, 55.
— of analogy, 62, 69.
— of hypothesis, 162.
— of law, 177.
Descartes, laws of refraction, 186 n.
Development hypothesis, 166.
— Mill quoted on, 166 n.
— Spencer quoted on, 167 n.
Dew, Wells's theory of, 21, 128.
Difference, canon of, 106.
— applications of, 107.
— proof of hypothesis, 173, 175.
Discovery by deduction, 144.
Distribution of natural law, 182.
Double agreement, canon of, 126.

Double agreement, 127, 128.

Effect, definition of, 27.
Effects, plurality of, maxim, 34.
— heterogeneous, 146.
— homogeneous, 147.
Efficient cause distinguished, 23 n.
Elimination, 25, 57, 92, 117, 121.
— Bacon on, 104 n.
Empirical truth, 10.
— view of causation, 31 n.
— certainty, 77, 83 n.
— laws of coexistence, 183.
— laws of succession, 185.
— laws becoming rational, 188.
Empiricism of Mill, 31 n., 67 n.
— of medical science, 186.
Energy, conservation of, 28, 196 n.
Enumeration, divided, 62.
— of cases, canon of, 63.
— value of, 66.
— Mill and Bacon on, 67 n.
— radical defect of, 102.
— of marks, canon of, 69.
— value of, 73.
Exceptions, 14, 80, 91, 95, 168.
Experience, inference from, 10, 54.
Experimental observation, 56, 107.
Explanation, philosophical, 190.

Familiarity *vs.* explanation, 190 n.
Force and energy, 27.
Formal character of logic, 1.
— of law, 178.
Forms, function of, 50, 107 n.

Generalization of induction, 5.
— from experience, 10.
— beyond experience, 14.
— within experience, 15.
— approximate, 81, 96.
Gravitation, universal, 175, 195.

Hamilton on induction, 6 n.
— on syllogistic form of, 46.
— on induction *vs.* deduction, 143 n.
Hazard, 15, 66, 73, 80, 94, 102, 139.
Herschel, on research, 105 n.
— on hazard of induction, 139 n.
— on induction *vs.* deduction, 142 n.

INDEX

Heterogeneous effects, 146.
Homogeneous effects, 147.
Hooker on obedience to law, 180 n.
Hypothesis, common use of, 155.
— Mill quoted on, 157 n.
— formal use of, 160.
— definition of, 162.
— of a *vera causa*, 163.
— of a *vera lex*, 165.
— of an ether, 164, 169, 171.
— of gases, kinetic, 165.
— of origin of species, 166.
— proof of, two steps, 171.
— of germs in disease, 173, 186.

Identification, 17, 145.
Imperfect induction, 45, 66, 102.
Induction a generalization, 5.
— definitions of, 6, 7 n.
— a synthetic process, 7.
— of accidents only, 9.
— exceptions, 14, 80, 91, 95, 168.
— perfect, 16, 45, 66 n., 102.
— preparation for, 20, 111, 121.
— principles of, 29.
— time not an element in, 42 n.
— an immediate inference, 43, 51.
— Aristotle's formula of, 44.
— Hamilton's syllogism, 46.
— Whately's and Mill's, 47.
— by enumeration, canon of, 63.
— by analogy, canon of, 69.
— perfect, general canon of, 103.
— quantitative, limits of, 138.
— *vs.* deduction, 142.
— of universal gravitation, 175.
Inductive logic formal, 1.
— sciences *vs.* deductive, 197.
Inference defined, 4.
— *a priori* and *a posteriori*, 12 n.
— inductive, immediate, 43, 51.
Instantia crucis, 168.
Intermixture of effects, 147, 149.
Intuitional view of causation, 30.
Intuitions, pure, distinguished, 11.

Kepler's laws, 18 n., 167, 174, 189.
Kinetic hypothesis of gases, 165.

Laplace on chance, 86.

Laplace's rule for probability, 124.
Law, definition of, 177, 178 n.
— formal and material, 178.
— moral and natural, 179, 182.
— misconceptions of, 180.
— derivative, 182, 185.
— empirical, 183, 185.
— rational, 187.
Laws of causation, 29.
— of motion, 31 n., 194.
— of light, 186 n.
— of liquid pressure, 188.
— of nature, 193.
— examples of, 194.
— ultimate number of, 199.
Leibnitz on sufficient reason, 85 n.
Limitations of the methods, 120.
— of quantitative induction, 138.
— of knowledge and power, 199 n.
— of natural law, 199.
Logic, definition of, 1.
— formal in both branches, 1.
— material *vs.* formal, 2 n.
— sole province of, 3.
Lotze on explanation, 192 n.

Mathematics, deductive, 13 n.
— applied to probabilities, 98.
— to concomitant variations, 135.
— inductions from, 138.
— in the deductive method, 152.
Metaphor *vs.* analogy, 68.
Method of difference, 104, 105.
— of residue, 112.
— of agreement, 104, 116.
— of double agreement, 125.
— of concomitant variations, 130.
— of deduction, 150.
Mill, material view of logic, 2 n.
— on induction *vs.* deduction, 5 n.
— definition of induction, 7 n.
— definition of cause, 27 n.
— empirical views of, 31 n., 67 n.
— inductive syllogism, 47 n.
— view of enumeration, 67 n.
— quoted on probability, 79, 95 n.
— canons of research, 105 n.
— on Darwin's hypothesis, 166 n.
— induction *vs.* deduction, 143 n.
— on law and cause, 182 n.

Mill on derivative laws, 189 n.
Montesquieu, law defined, 178 n.
— on obedience to law, 181 n.
Moral certainty, 77, 83 n.

Natural law *vs.* moral law, 179.
— distribution of, 182.
Nature, laws of, 193.
— of motion, 31 n., 194.
— of gravitation, 195.
— of energy, 196.
— of chemical combination, 197.
— number of, ultimate, 199.
Neptune, discovery of, 20.
Newton's laws of motion, 31 n., 194.
— rules for philosophizing, 36 n.
— deductive method, 154.
— doctrine of *vera causa*, 163 n.
— hypothetical method, 174.
— hypothesis of light, 168.
— law of gravitation, 175, 195.

Observation, definition of, 55.
— simple, applications, 57, 107.
— experimental, 59, 109.
Order, logical *vs.* historical, 153 n.
Organum, as a title, 142 n.

Parcimony, law of, 36 n.
Pascal's law of pressure, 188.
Perfect induction, 16, 45, 66 n., 102.
Phenomenon, definition of, 54.
— of coexistence, 54, 183.
— of succession, 55, 185.
Philosophizing, rules for, 36 n.
Physical certainty, 77, 83 n.
Plurality of effects, 34, 123.
— of causes, 37, 122.
Prediction, power of, 170.
Preventive cause, 25, 81, 109 n.
Primeval agents, 184 n., 189.
Probability, canon of, 89.
— indefinite valuation of, 94.
— numerical valuation of, 98.
— based on statistics, 100.
— Laplace's rule for, 124.

Proof of an hypothesis, 171.
Pure logic divided, 1.
— intuitions distinguished, 11.
— mathematics, deductive, 13 n.

Quantitative inductions, 138.

Rational law, 182, 187.
Residue, method of, 112.
— canon of, 113.
— applications of, 114.
Rules for philosophizing, 36 n.

Sciences, quantitative, 135.
— becoming deductive, 197.
Spencer on evolution, 167 n.
Statistics, application of, 100.
Sufficient reason, axiom of, 85.
Syllogism of induction, 44.
— Hamilton's, 46.
— Whately's and Mill's, 47.
— objections to, 48.
Synthesis of induction, 7.

Theory *vs.* hypothesis, 165 n.
— how established, 171.

Uniformity of nature, 39.
— of coexistence, 54, 183.
— of succession, 55, 185.

Variations, concomitant, 130.
— canon of, 131.
— illustrations of, 132.
— quantitative estimates, 137.
Venn on Mill, 2 n., 27 n., 38 n.
Vera causa and *lex*, 163, 165.
Verification, 145, 152.
— special function of, 169.
— predictions not proof, 170.

Wells, research on dew, 21, 128.
Whately, induction defined, 6 n.
— inductive syllogism, 47.
Whewell on induction, 6 n.
— on Supreme Cause, 193 n.

FINIS

STANDARD EDUCATIONAL WORKS.

DAVIS'S DEDUCTIVE LOGIC.
The Elements of Deductive Logic. By NOAH K. DAVIS, Ph.D., LL.D., Professor of Moral Philosophy in the University of Virginia. Cloth, 90 cents.

I am not acquainted with any treatise on logic that contains within the same compass so much sound logical doctrine so perspicuously expressed as the "Elements of Deductive Logic." . . . It would not be difficult to point out in this small work at least half a dozen distinct gains to the science.—Professor COLLINS DENNY, Vanderbilt University, Nashville, Tenn.

DAVIS'S THEORY OF THOUGHT.
The Theory of Thought. A Treatise on Deductive Logic. By NOAH K. DAVIS, University of Virginia. 8vo, Cloth, $2 00.

A comprehensive account of the science of logic from its earliest days, with every variety of example to illustrate the principles. . . . The author is to be commended for his industry, his earnestness, his intelligence in the arrangement of his material, and the general excellence of his literary style.—*Philadelphia Bulletin.*

HILL'S RHETORIC.
The Principles of Rhetoric, and their Application. By ADAMS SHERMAN HILL, Boylston Professor of Rhetoric and Oratory in Harvard College. With an Appendix comprising General Rules for Punctuation. 12mo, Half Leather, 80 cents.

We commend the book to all educators of youth, and we particularly advise those who are seeking to educate themselves in English composition to make a thorough study of its pages.—*Christian at Work*, N. Y.

HILL'S OUR ENGLISH.
Our English. By ADAMS SHERMAN HILL, Boylston Professor of Rhetoric and Oratory in Harvard University. 16mo, Cloth, $1 00. [*Sent by mail on receipt of price.*]

Professor Hill is an acknowledged authority upon the use of our language. In this work he gives chapters on English in schools, in colleges, in newspapers and novels, in the pulpit, and on colloquial English.

HILL'S FOUNDATIONS OF RHETORIC.

The Foundations of Rhetoric. By ADAMS SHERMAN HILL. 12mo, Cloth, $1 00.

It is a rich and ingenious book. A subject usually reckoned dry and intricate here becomes, by means of neat arrangement and a mass of admirably selected illustrations, luminous and even entertaining. Hereafter clumsiness in writing will be more discreditable than before.—Professor G. H. PALMER, Harvard University.

I do not like to write opinions of text-books in ordinary cases, but this book is so full of valuable devices to develop in the student a critical knowledge of the best usages of an English style that I am very glad to say a word commending it to all schools seeking a good text-book in English composition. — Hon. W. T. HARRIS, U. S. Commissioner of Education.

BOWNE'S PSYCHOLOGICAL THEORY.

Introduction to Psychological Theory. By BORDEN P. BOWNE. 8vo, Cloth, $1 75.

This is not a dogmatic treatise of empirical psychology, much less a digest of physiological psychology and the fanciful theories that cluster round that shadowy border-land of research, but a series of essays in pure psychology, the basis of the whole performance being facts, not theories.—*Boston Beacon.*

BOWNE'S METAPHYSICS.

Metaphysics. A Study in First Principles. By BORDEN P. BOWNE. 8vo, Cloth, $1 75.

Will mark an era in the discussion between materialists and intuitionalists, and between sceptics and theistic believers.... To read this thoughtful volume will be a wholesome intellectual discipline, as well as a strong confirmation of faith in revealed religion as the true philosophy of the universe and of man.—*Zion's Herald*, Boston.

BOWNE'S PHILOSOPHY OF THEISM.

Philosophy of Theism. By BORDEN P. BOWNE. 8vo, Cloth, $1 75.

Professor Bowne is widely known to students of philosophy by his masterly and lucid treatises on metaphysics, studies in Theism, psychology, etc. He is an acute and original thinker, and a profound logician.... Materialism has one of its most forceful opponents in Professor Bowne, whose writings furnish strong confirmation of faith in revealed religion.—*Albany Press.*

THE PRINCIPLES OF ETHICS.

By BORDEN P. BOWNE, Professor of Philosophy in Boston University. 8vo, Cloth, $1 75.

This work is designed to be not so much a detailed discussion of specific duties and virtues as an introduction to fundamental moral ideas and principles. While demonstrating the necessity of uniting the intuitive and the experience school of ethics in order to reach any working system, the author seeks to show that the aim of conduct is not abstract virtue, but fulness and richness of life. The work is marked throughout by that profundity of thought and clearness of expression which have made Professor Bowne's earlier works so successful. No pains has been spared to make it as perfect as possible.

DEWEY'S PSYCHOLOGY.

Psychology. By JOHN DEWEY, Ph.D. 12mo, Cloth $1 25.

It avoids all material not strictly psychological, and embodies the results of the latest investigations. . . . It is a successful effort to treat psychology scientifically by itself as an introduction to the study of philosophy in general. It is learned and strict in its method, both analysis and definition are clear, and the subject is developed well to make principles and their application readily understood by thoughtful students.—*Boston Globe.*

As a philosophical text-book its claims to the recognition of thinkers are very great, while as an exposition of one of the most interesting of sciences, it will be a hand-book of inestimable value to students. —*Commonwealth,* Boston.

MILL'S LOGIC: REVISED EDITION.

A System of Logic, Ratiocinative and Inductive: being a Connected View of the Principles of Evidence and the Methods of Scientific Investigation. By JOHN STUART MILL. Printed from the Eighth London Edition. 8vo, Cloth, $2 50. [*Sent by mail on receipt of price.*]

Those who choose to grapple with this work will find that it presents a new view of the subject; that it is a sort of "Novum Organum," adapted to the state of intellectual and physical science at the present day; and that it is treated with a breadth and comprehensiveness of thought, in a style of thorough analysis, and with a surpassingly clear and forcible diction which entitle it to the study of all who aspire to the merit of philosophical research or even of general scholarship.—*North American Review.*

Standard Educational Works.

HAVEN'S RHETORIC.

Rhetoric: a Text-book, designed for Use in Schools and Colleges, and for Private Study. By the Rev. E. O. HAVEN, D.D., LL.D. 12mo, Cloth, 90 cents.

We find that the good opinion we had formed of it, on the strength of the author's reputation, was not up to its actual merits. The science and art of Rhetoric seem to have been mastered by President Haven as never before by any writer upon Rhetoric.—*Chicago Journal.*

JOHNSON'S ENGLISH WORDS.

An Elementary Study of Derivations. By CHARLES F. JOHNSON, Professor of English Literature, Trinity College, Hartford. 16mo, Cloth, 84 cents.

Modest in size, but packed from cover to cover with information about the history of words used in the English of to-day.—*Rochester Herald.*

Pretty certain to lead the way to a more serious study of our language, not only in the school but in the home circle as well, its modest size and untechnical character strongly commending it for the latter use.—*Southern Educator,* Durham, N. C.

WHATELY'S LOGIC.

Elements of Logic. Comprising the Substance of the Article in the Encyclopædia Metropolitana. With Additions, etc. By RICHARD WHATELY, D.D., late Archbishop of Dublin. 18mo, Cloth, 50 cents.

WHATELY'S RHETORIC.

Elements of Rhetoric. Comprising an Analysis of the Laws of Moral Evidence and of Persuasion. With Rules of Argumentative Composition and Elocution. By RICHARD WHATELY, D.D., late Archbishop of Dublin. 18mo, Cloth, 50 cents.

PUBLISHED BY HARPER & BROTHERS, NEW YORK.

The above works are for sale by all booksellers, or will be sent by the publishers on receipt of price. If ordered sent by mail, 10 per cent. must be added to cover cost of postage, unless otherwise indicated.

www.ingramcontent.com/pod-product-compliance
Lightning Source LLC
Chambersburg PA
CBHW020815230426
43666CB00007B/1025